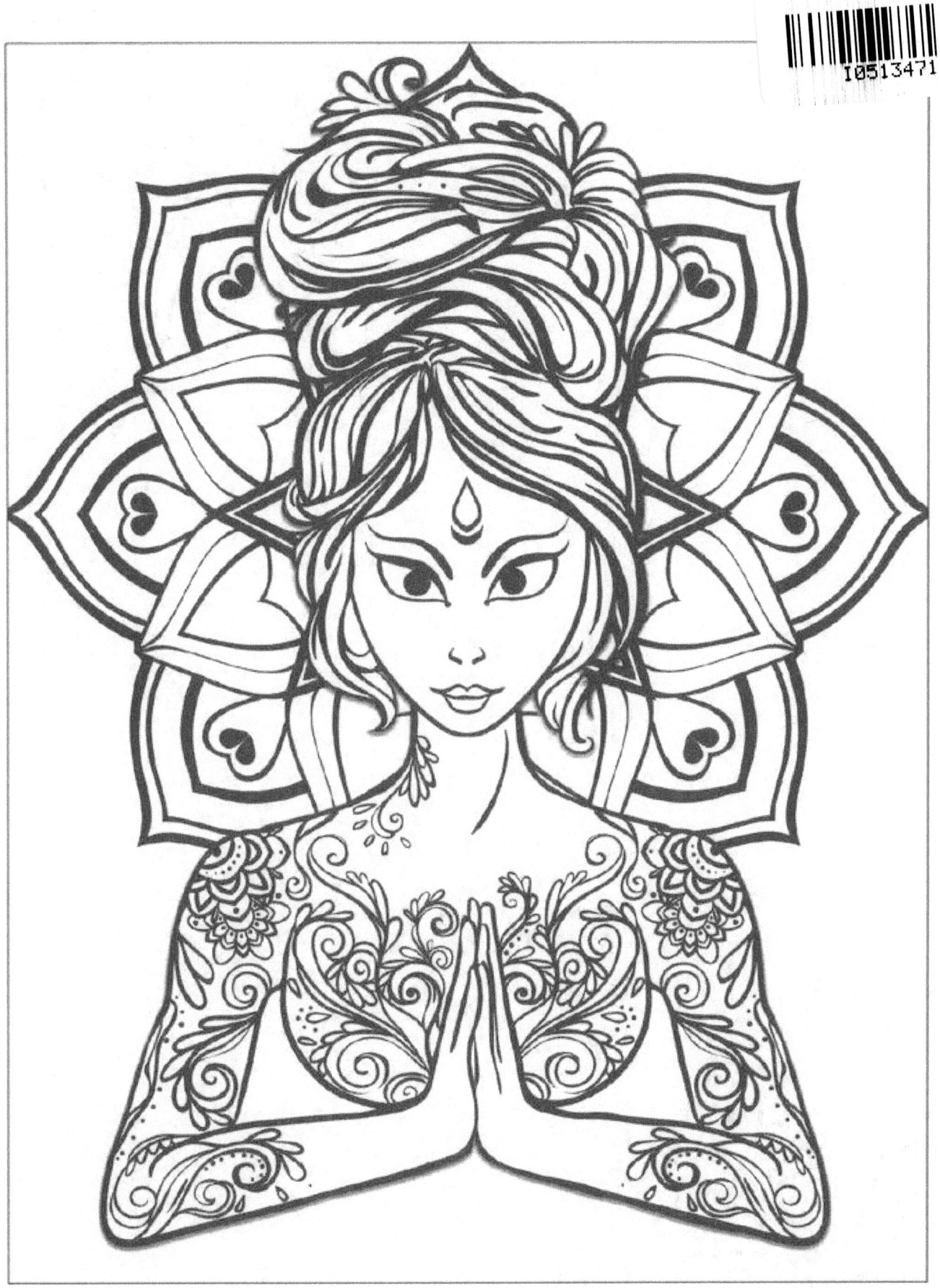

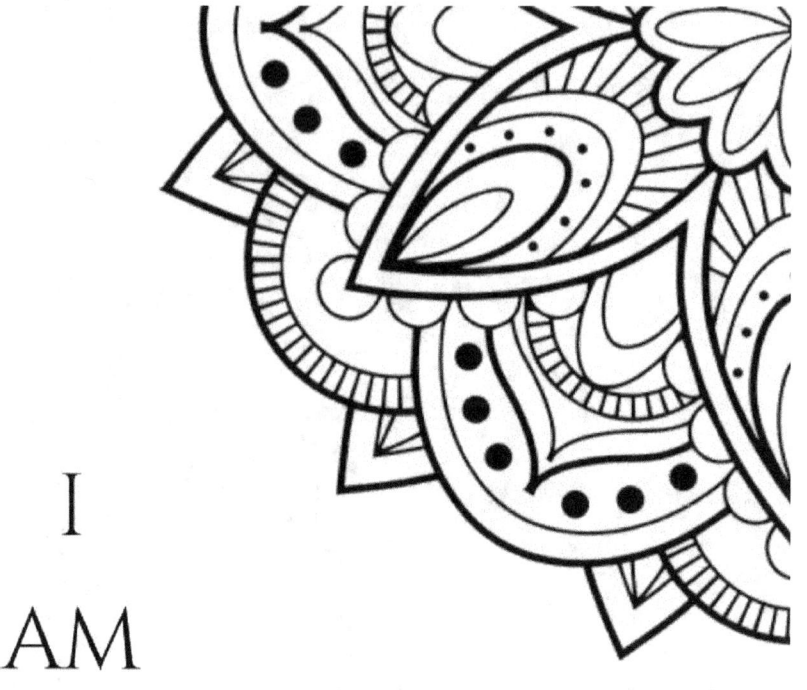

I
AM
PEACEFUL
IN THE
PRESENCE
OF
CHOAS

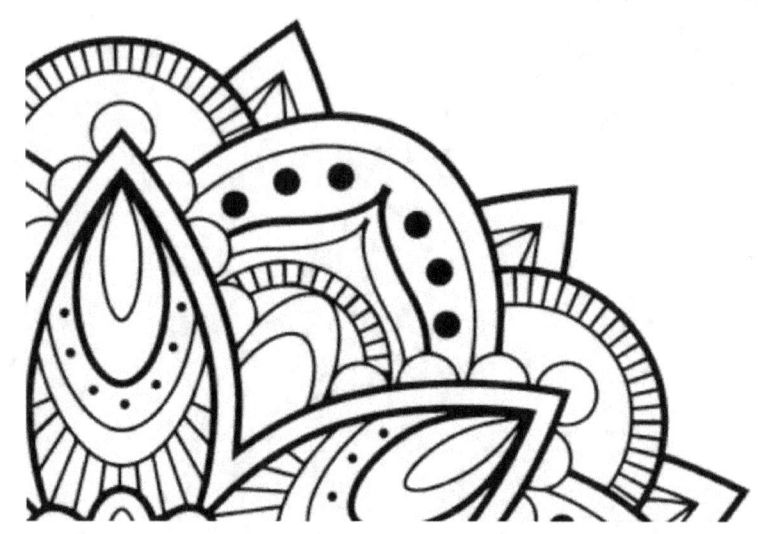

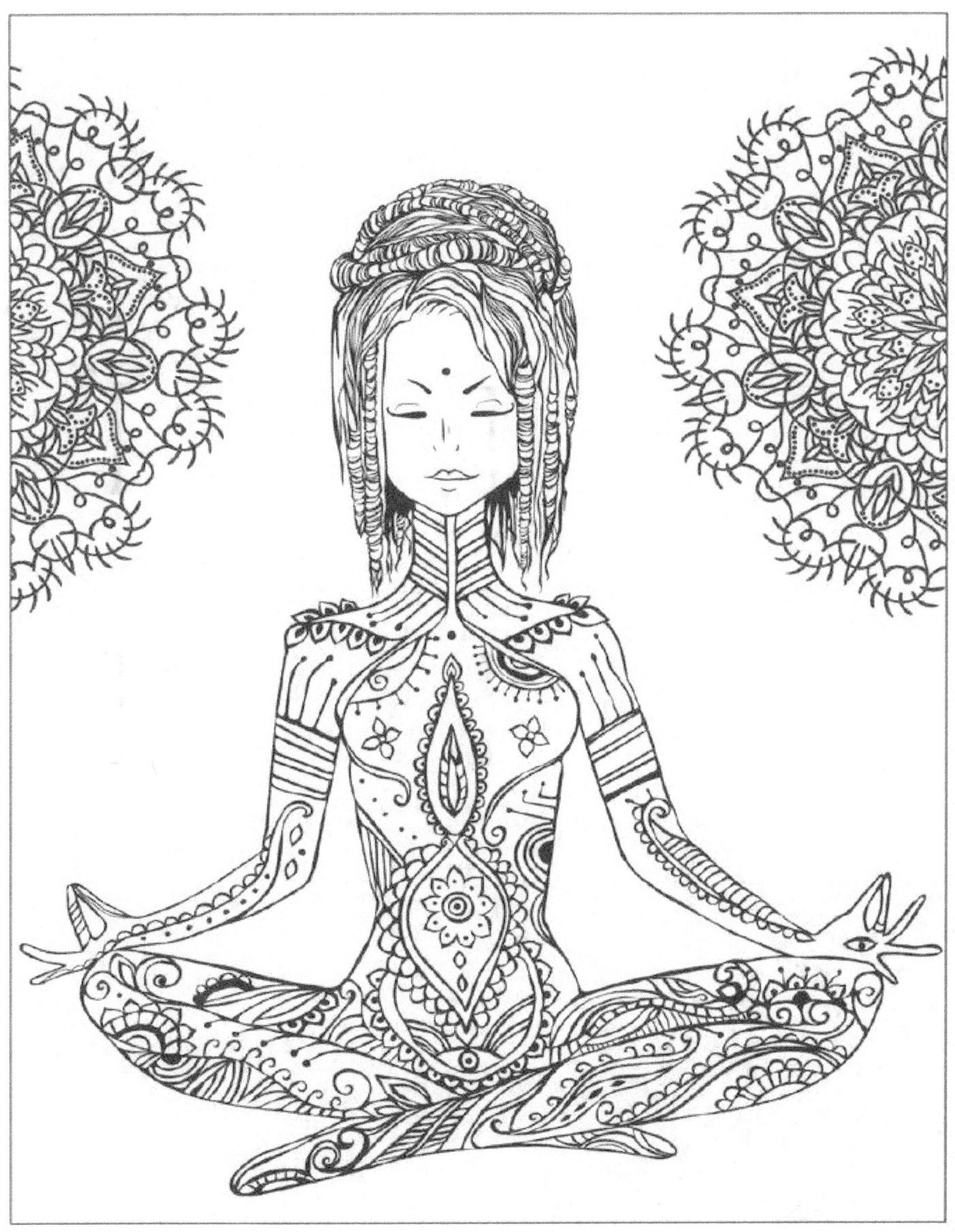

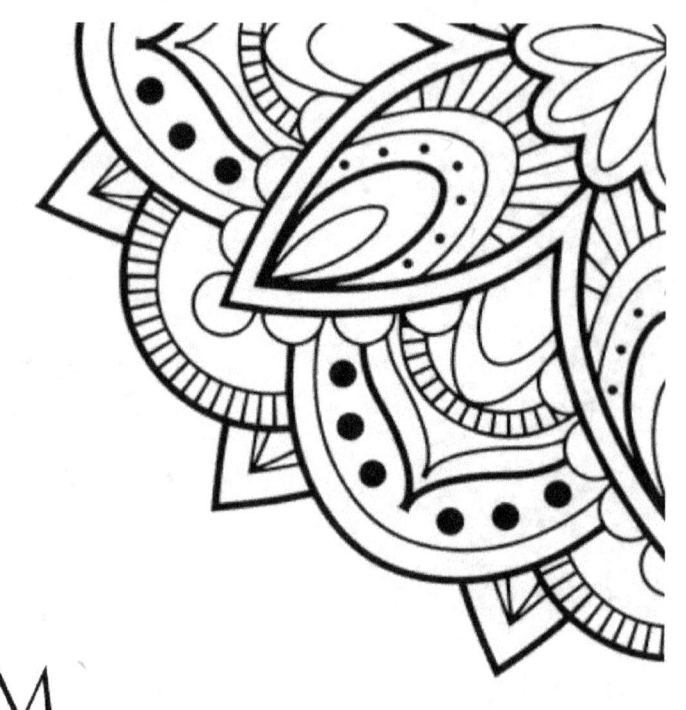

I AM
SURROUNDED
BY
ABUNDANCE
AND
PROSPERITY

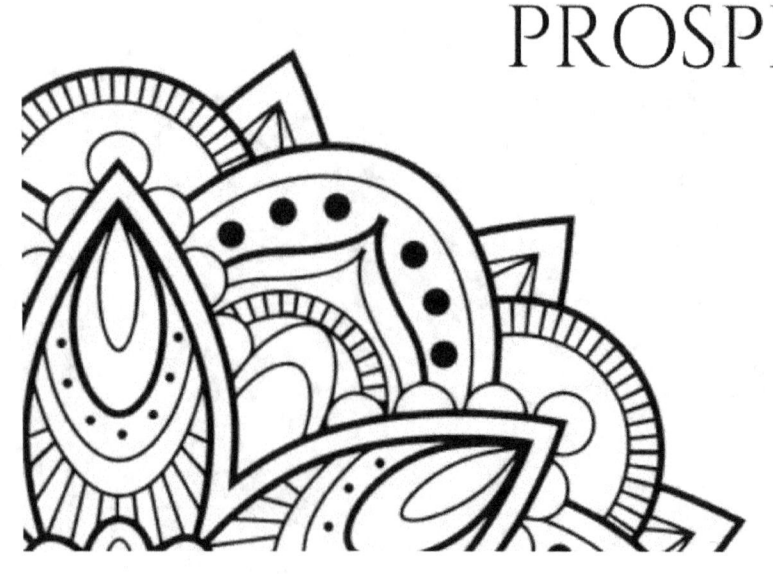

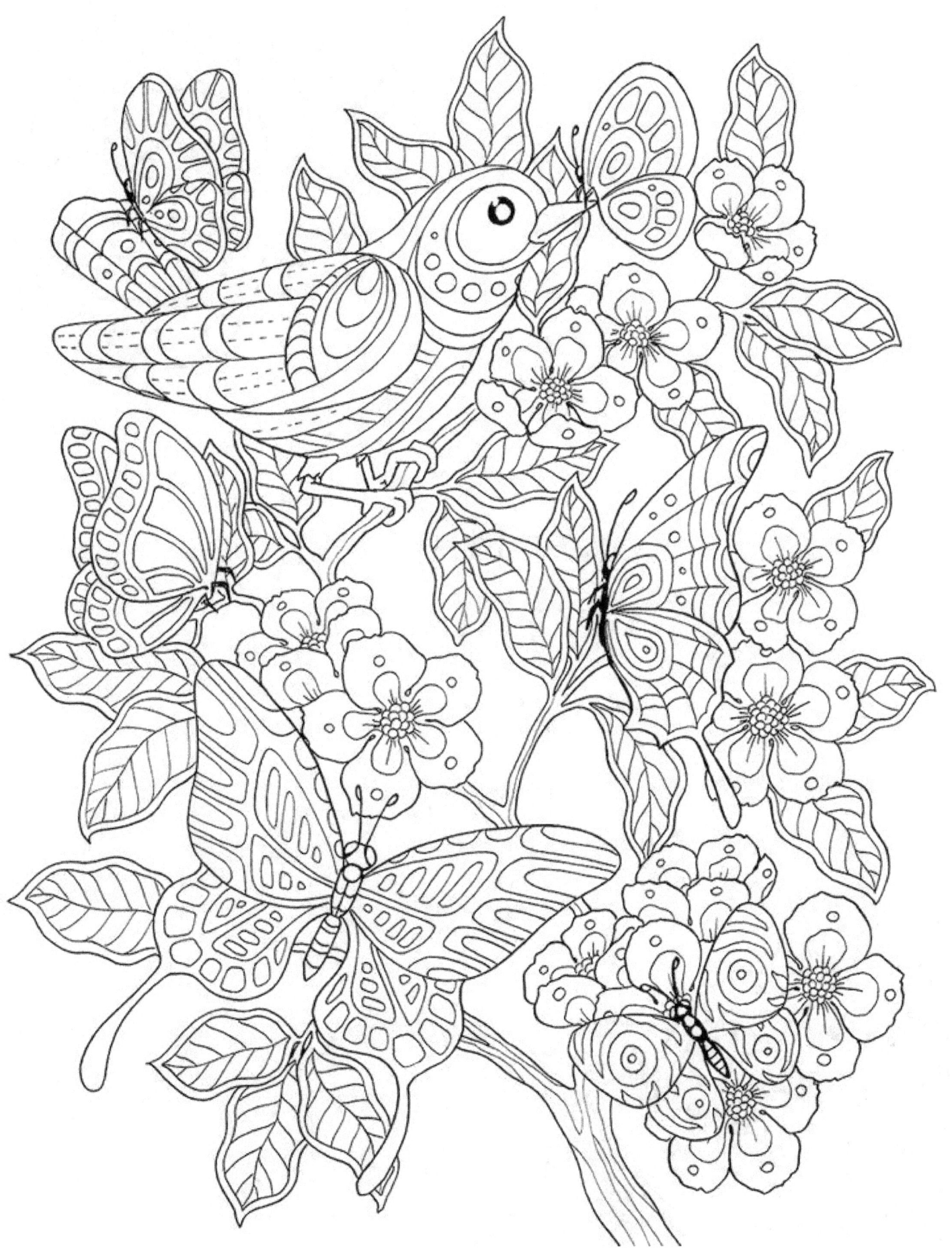

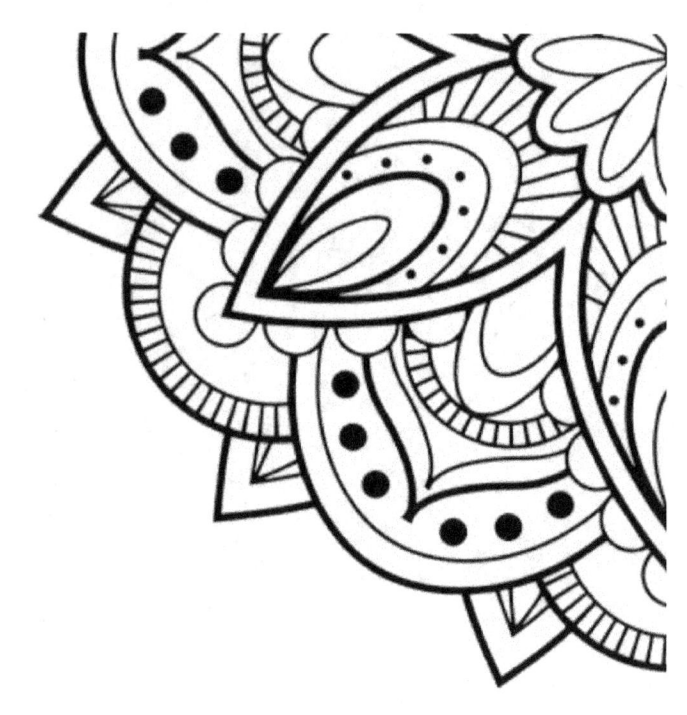

ANYTHING IS
POSSIBLE
WITH A
PLAN

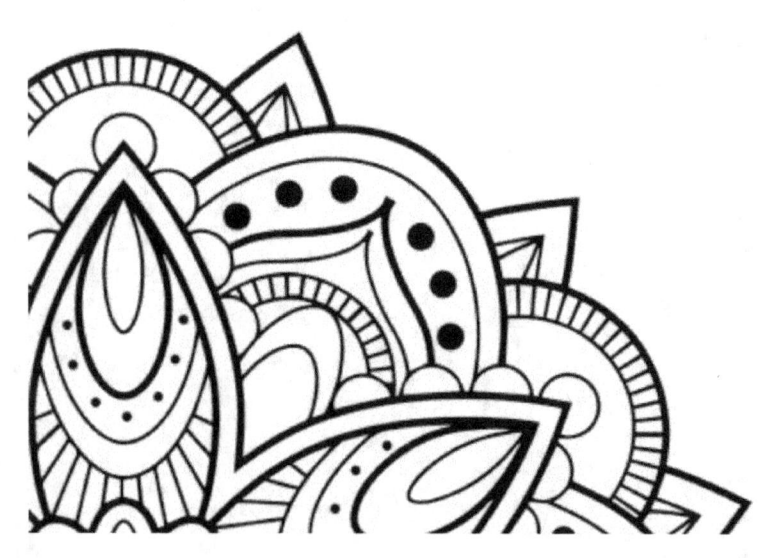

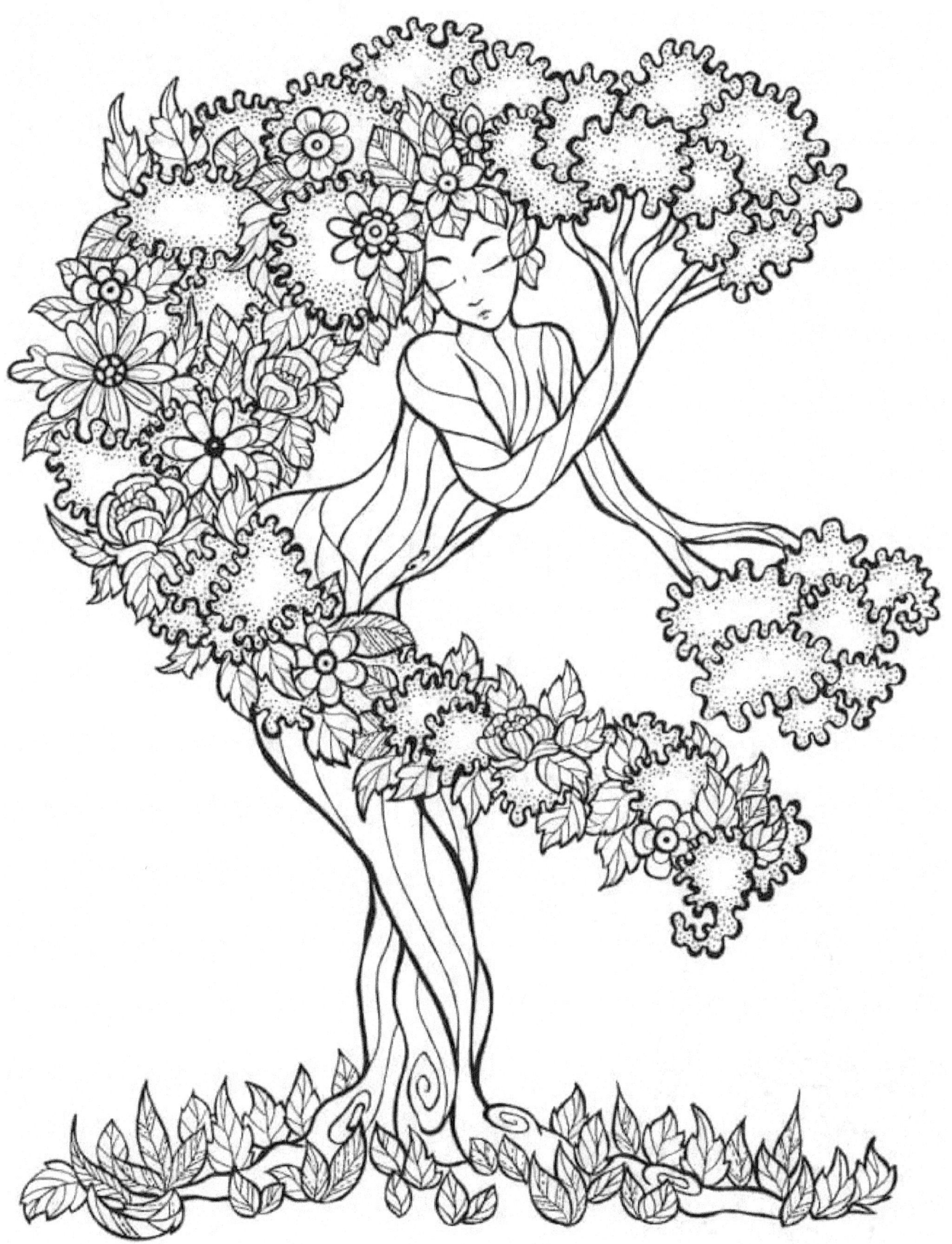

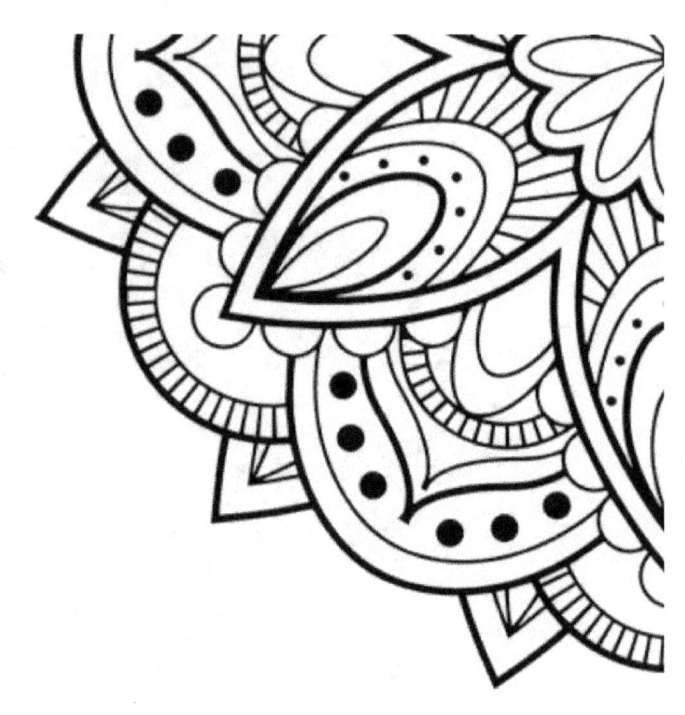

KINDNESS

IS

FREE

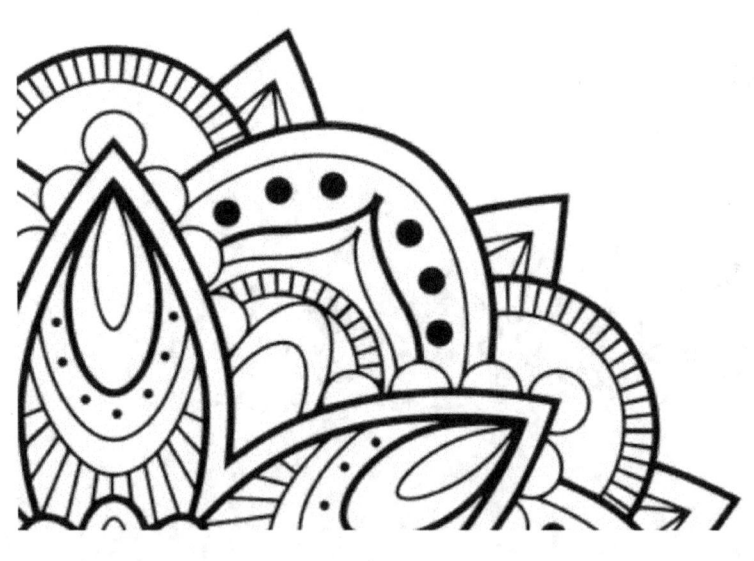

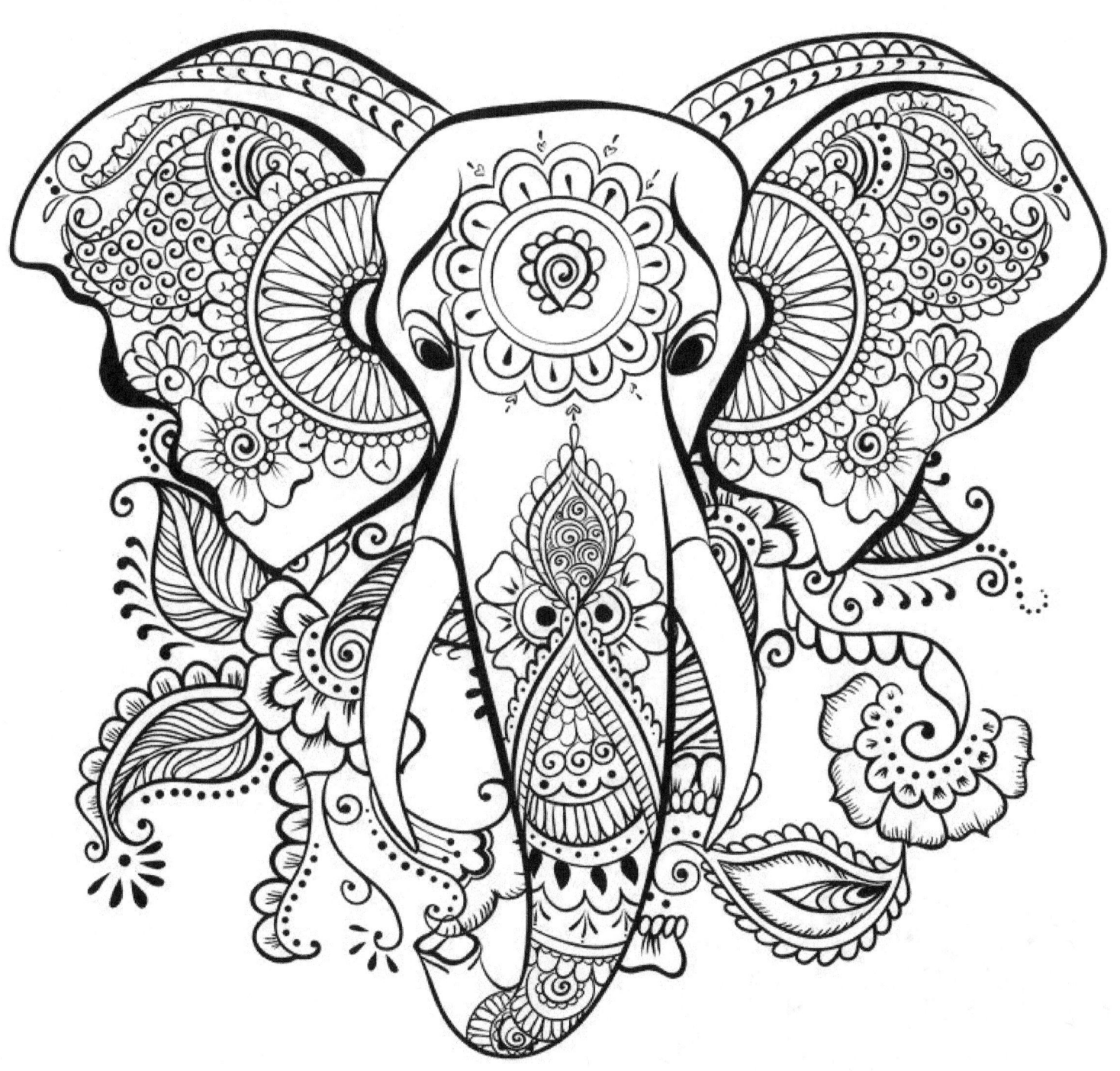

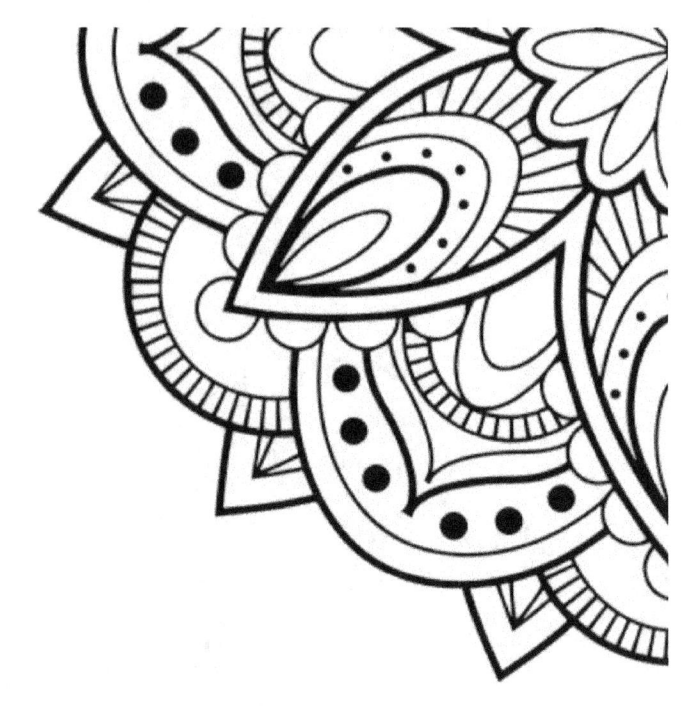

As I exhale, stress leaves my body

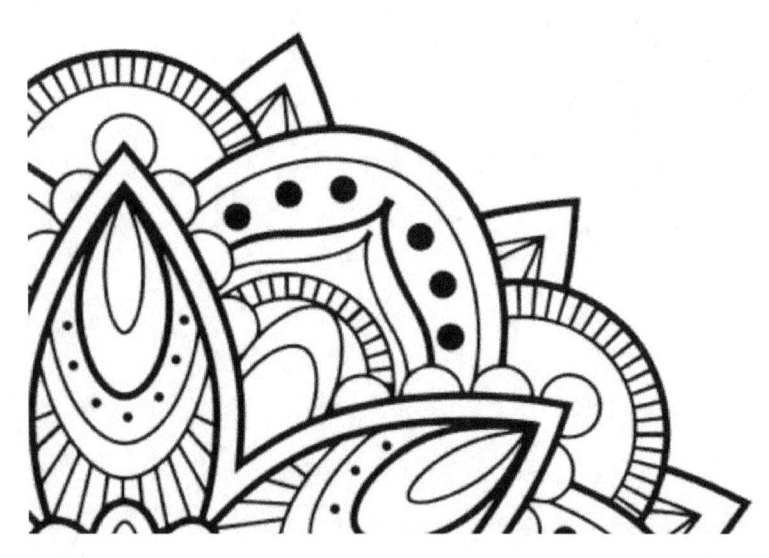

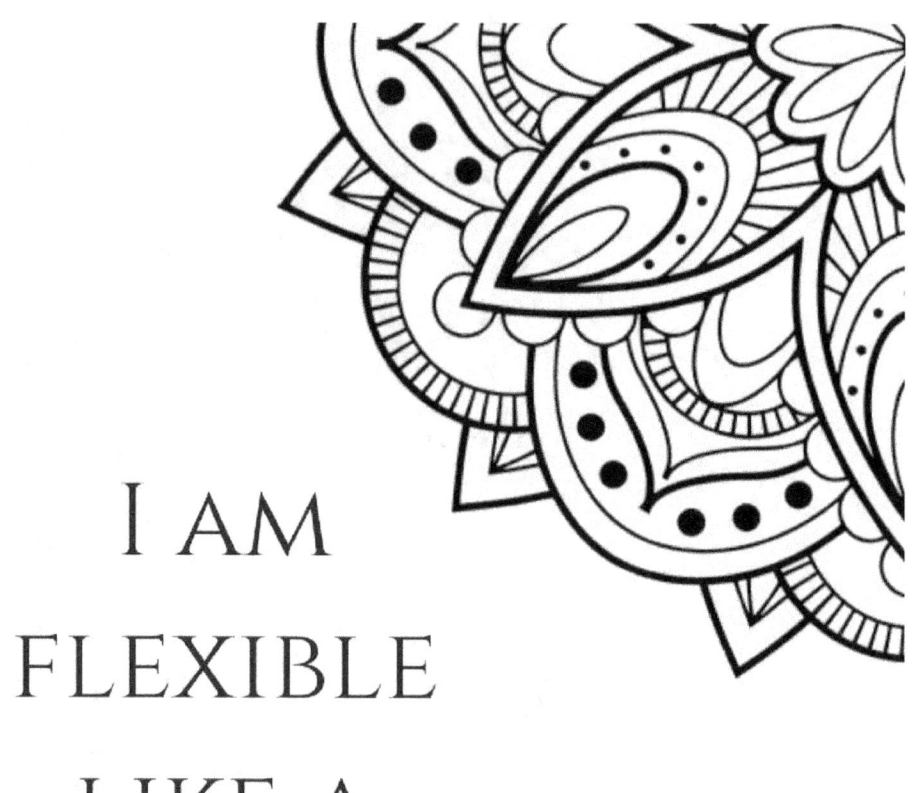

I AM
FLEXIBLE
LIKE A
SPRING,
BENDING
BUT NOT
BREAKING

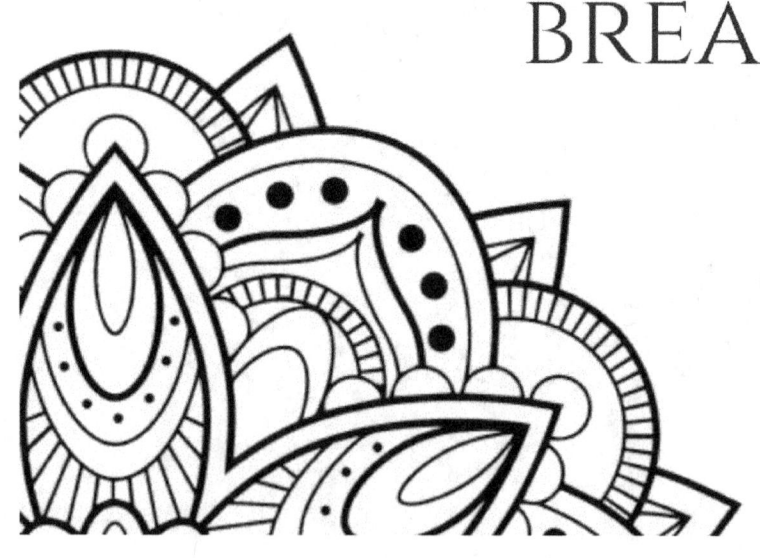

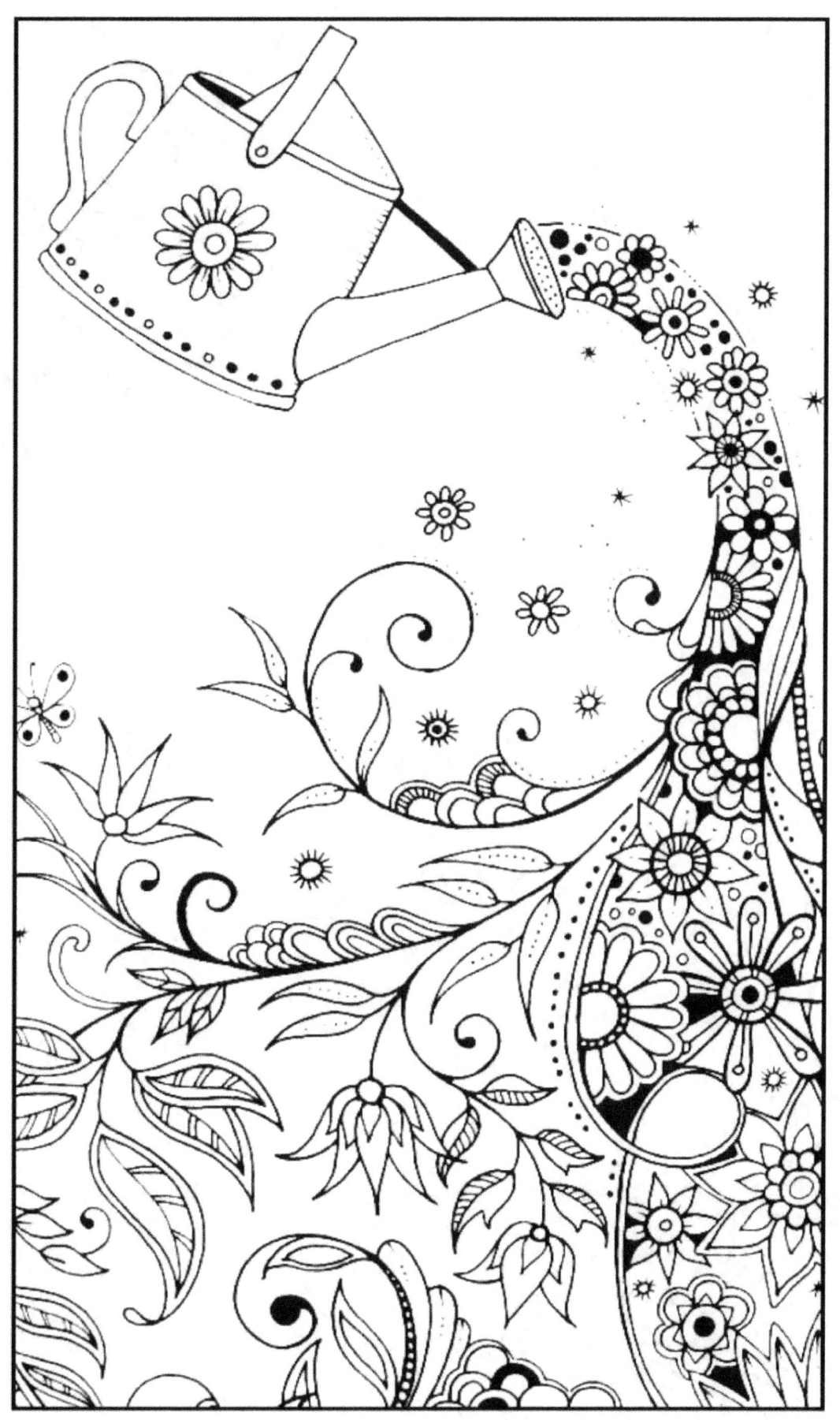

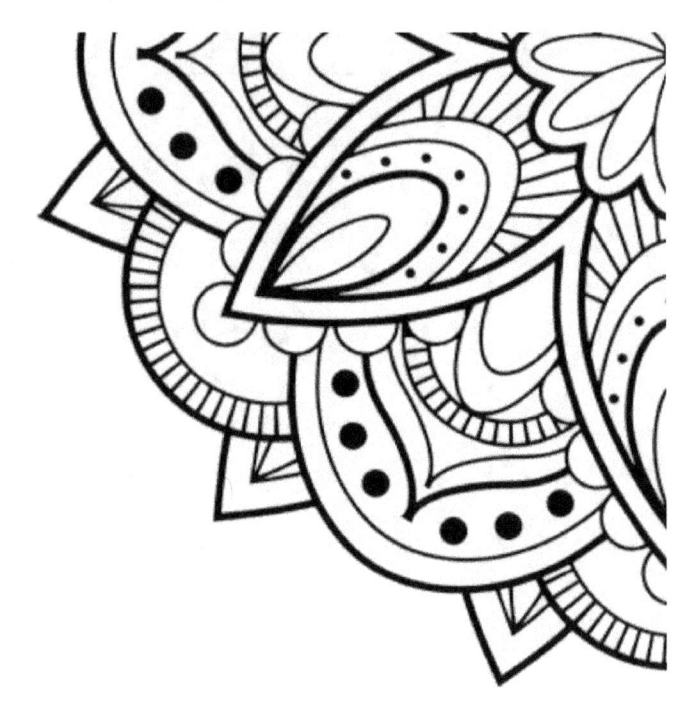

MY PEACE
IS MY
POWER

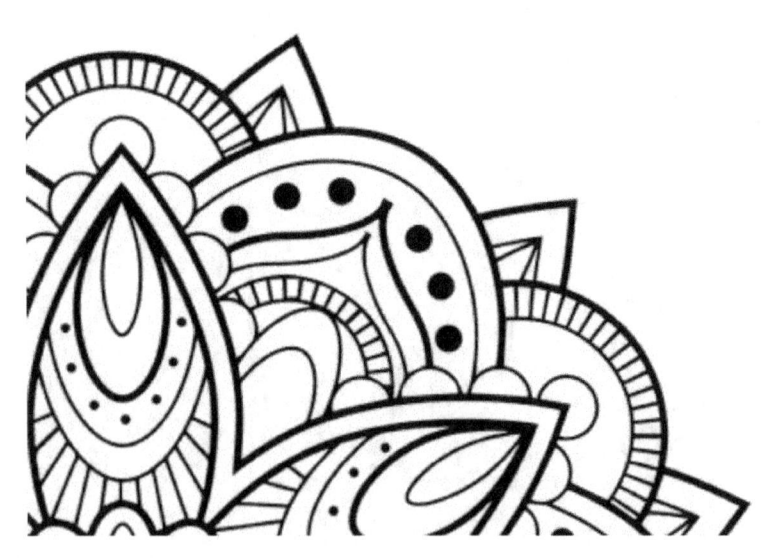

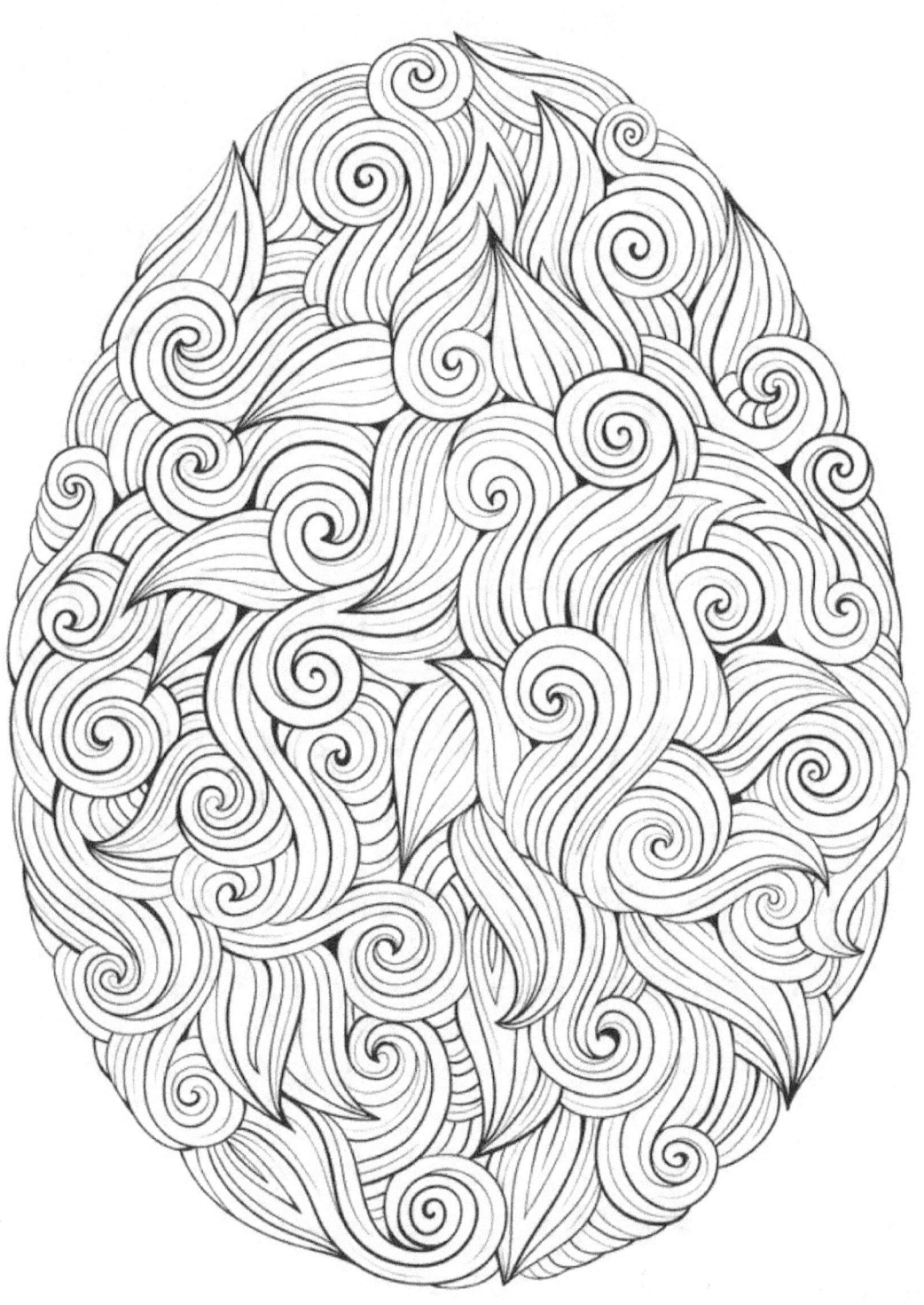

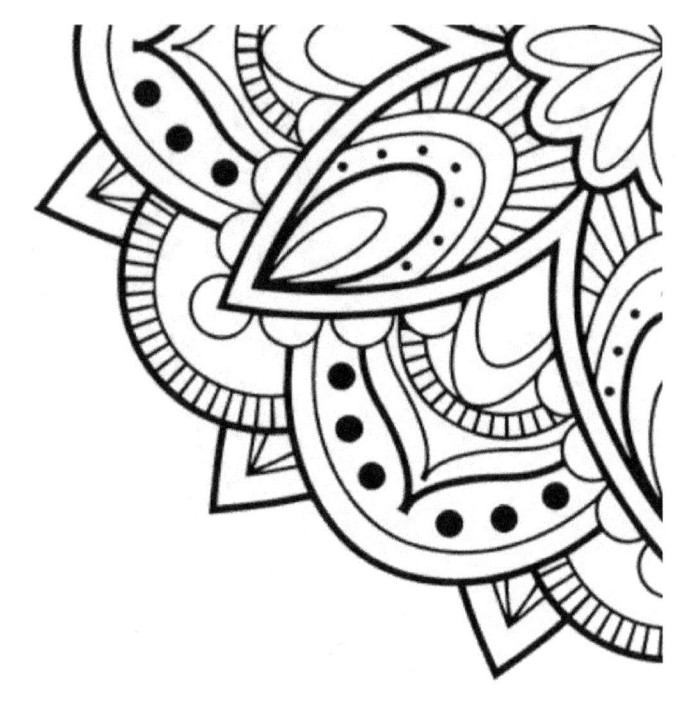

I

RECLAIM

MY OWN

POWER

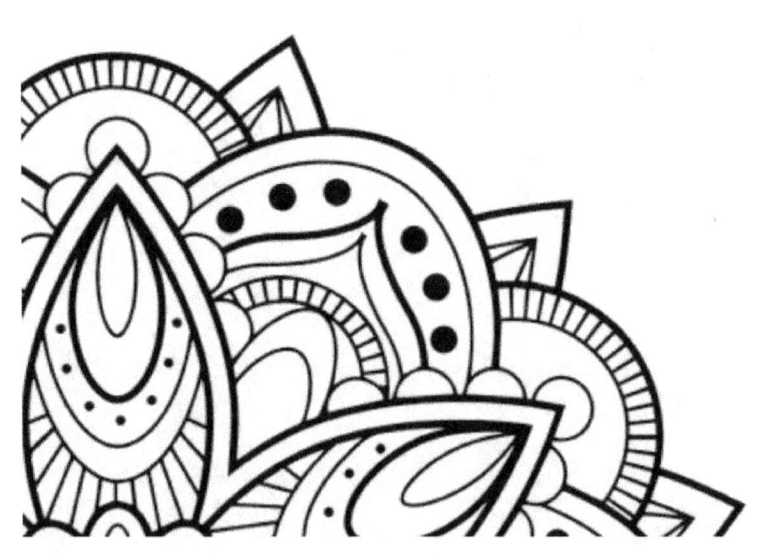

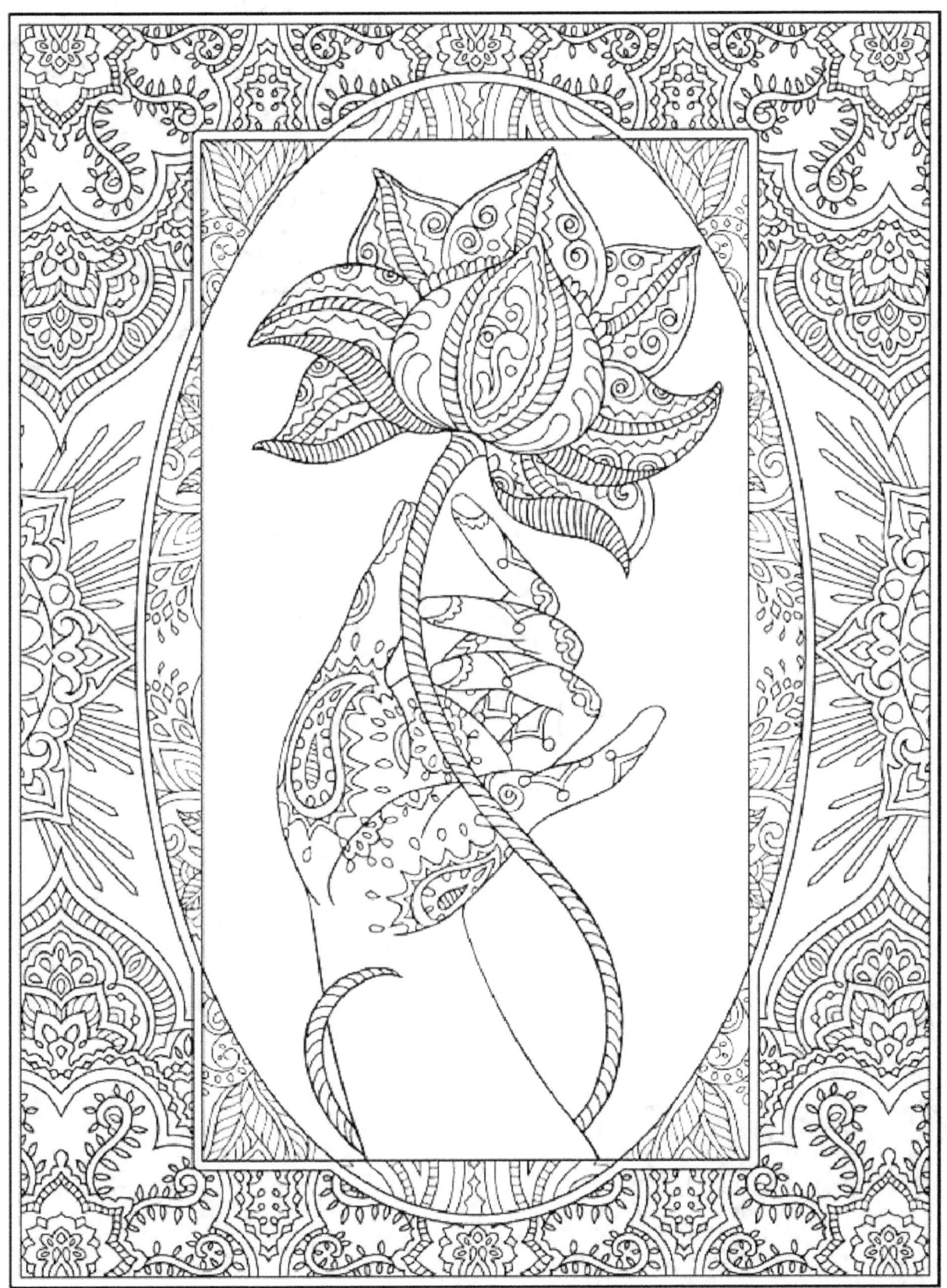

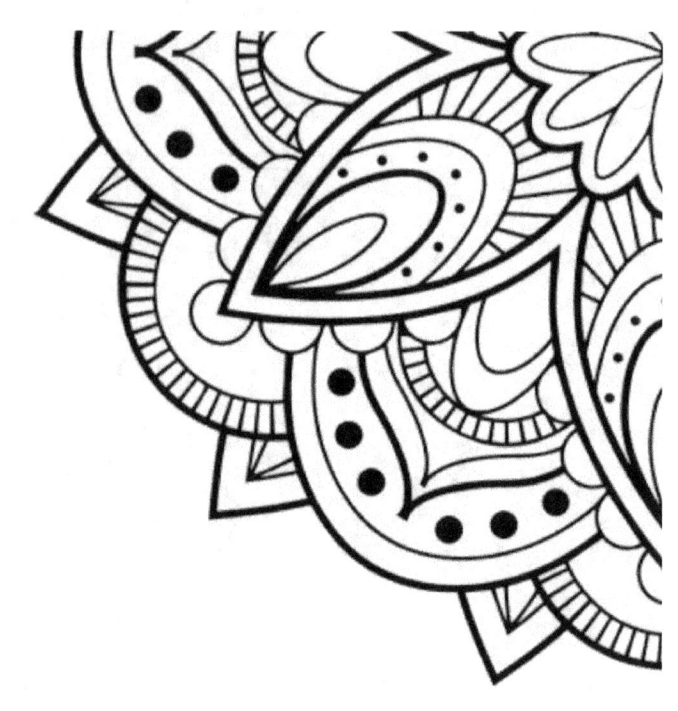

I DON'T SWEAT
THE SMALL
STUFF

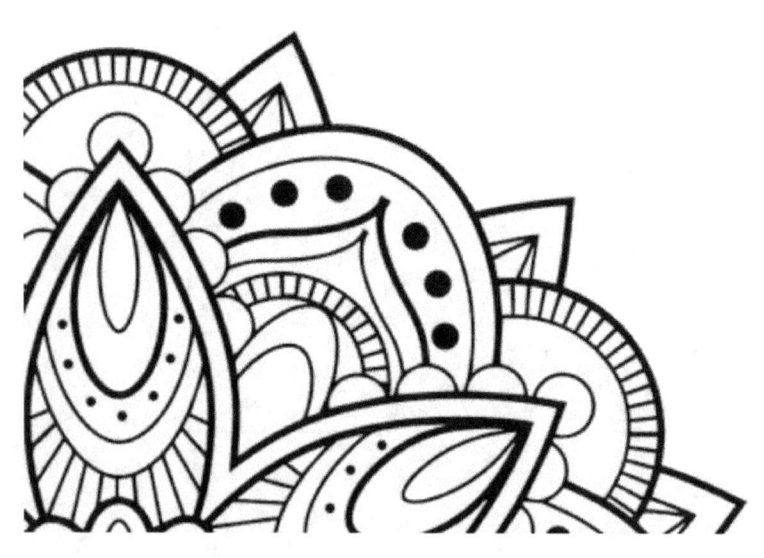

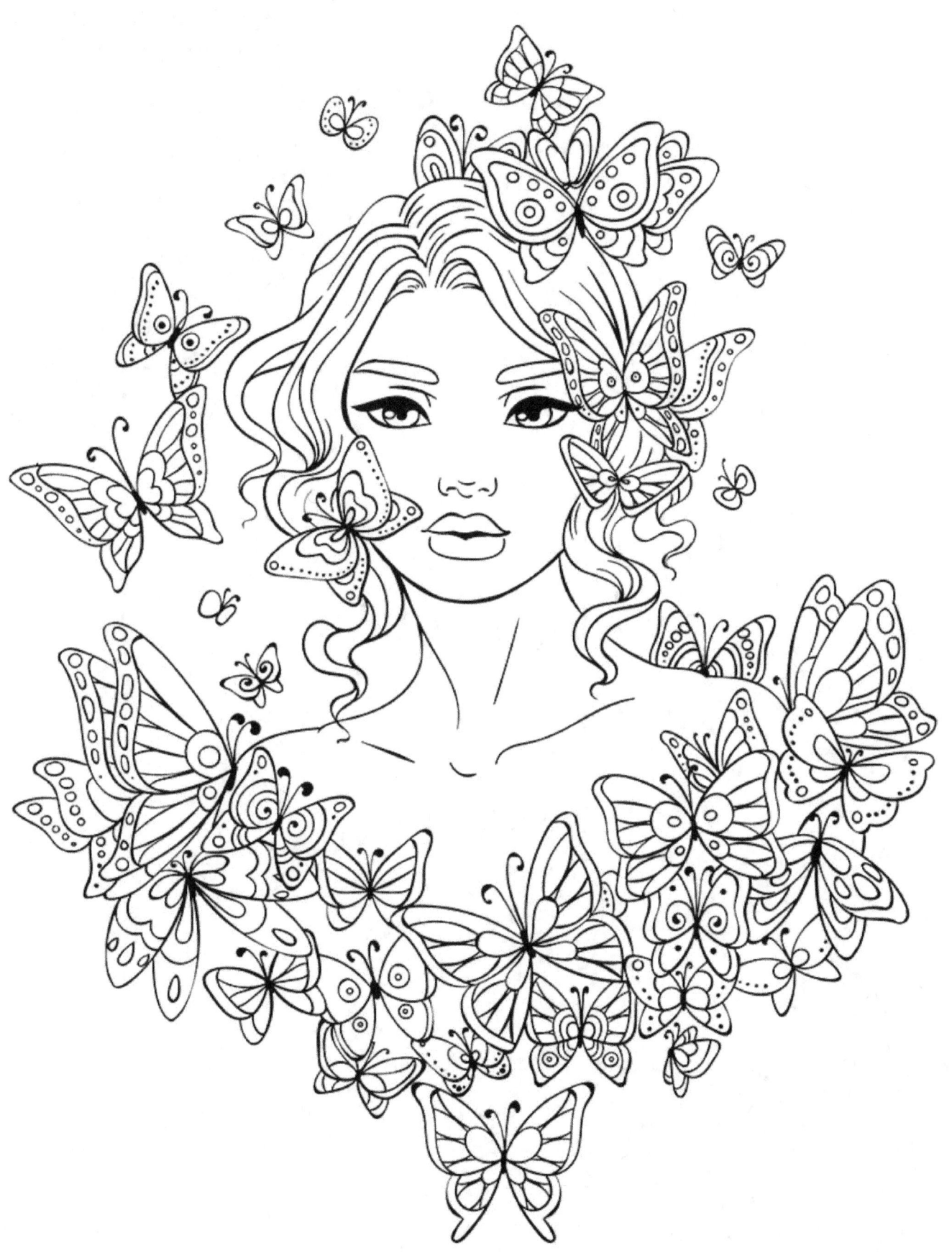

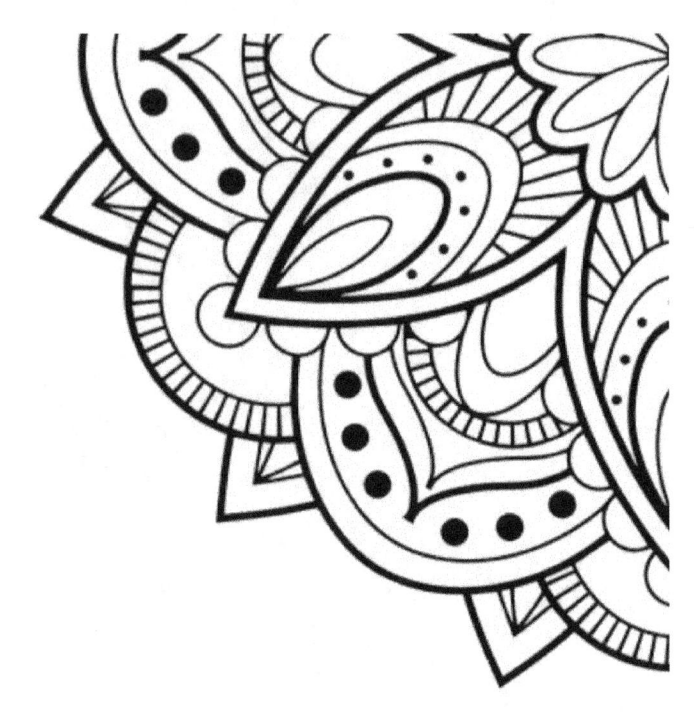

I FEED MY SPIRIT

I TRAIN MY BODY

I FOCUS MY MIND

IT'S MY TIME

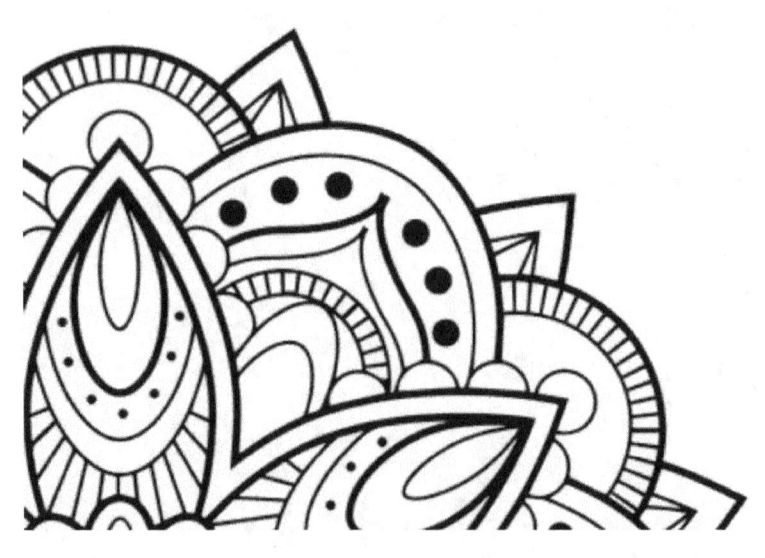

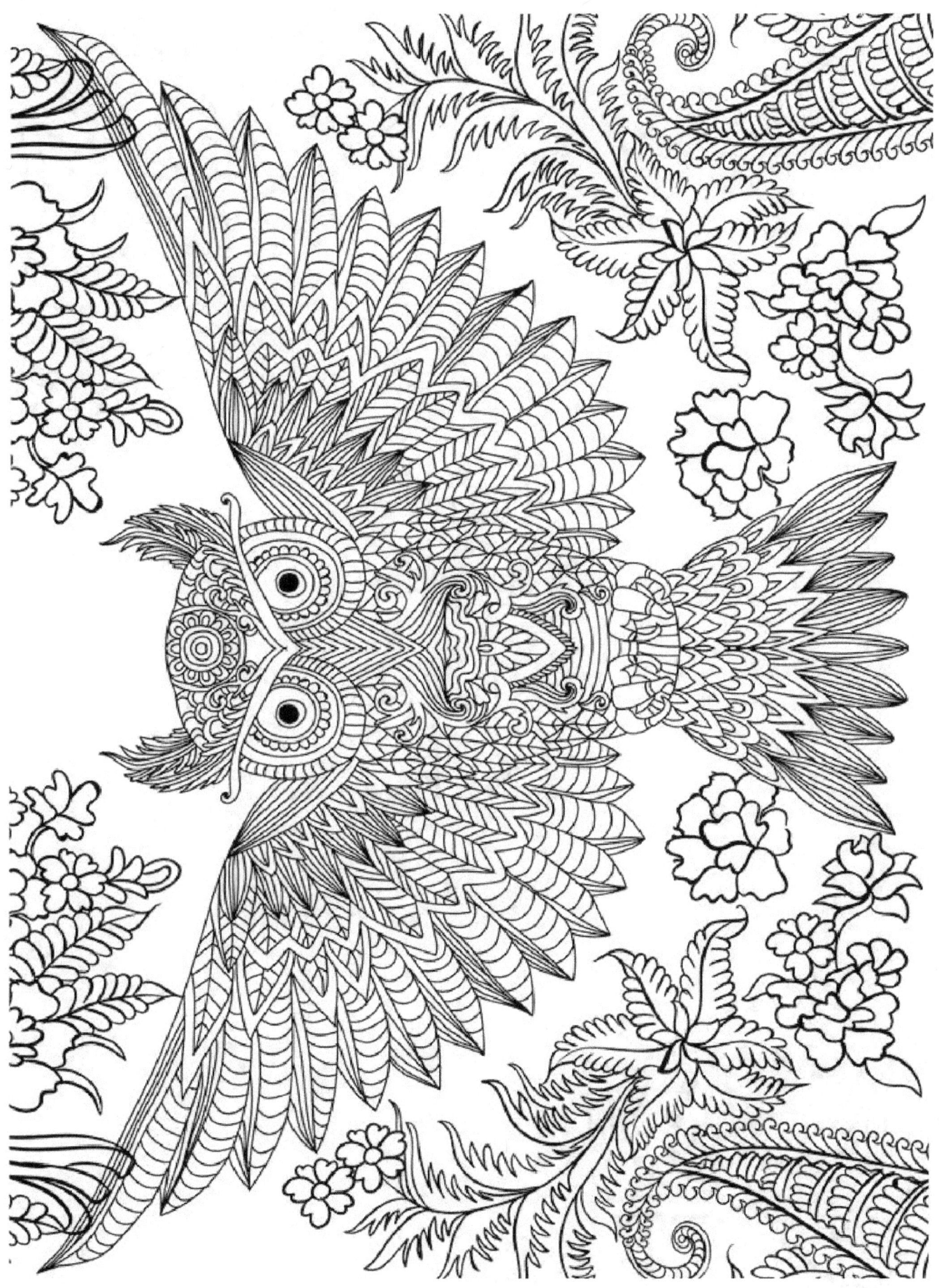

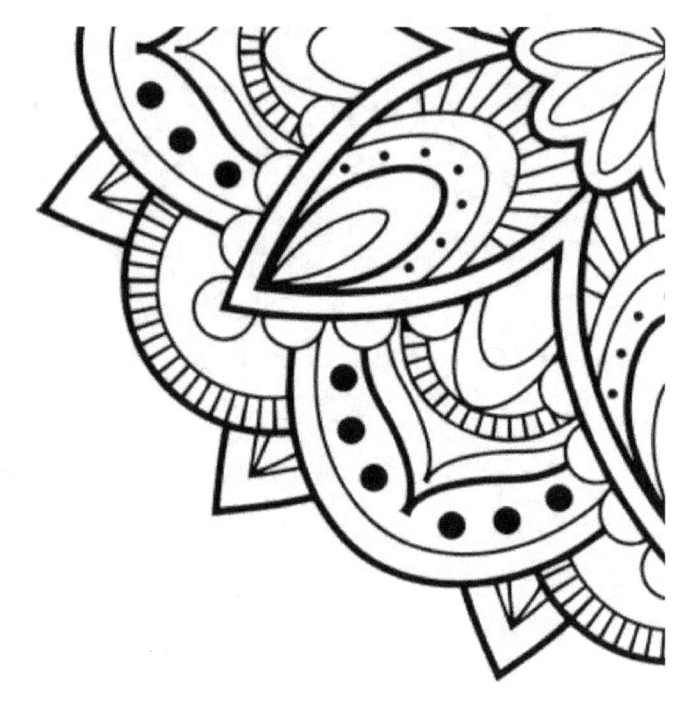

I AM A
SURGE OF
CREATIVE
ENERGY

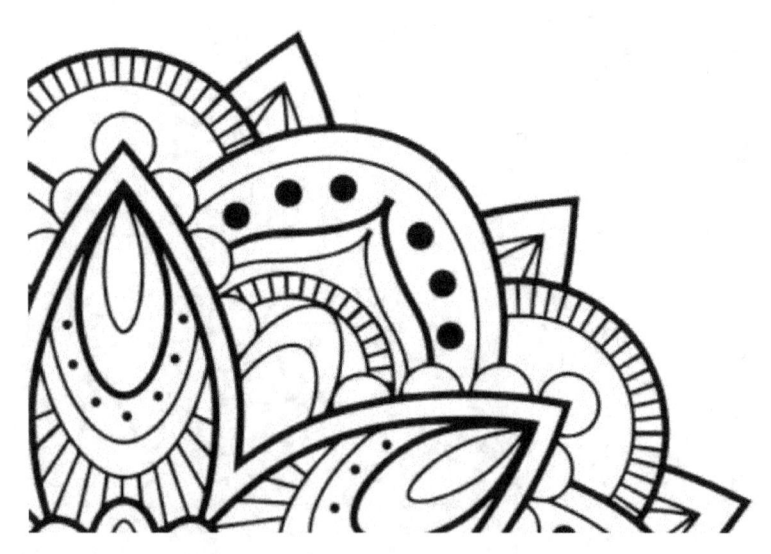

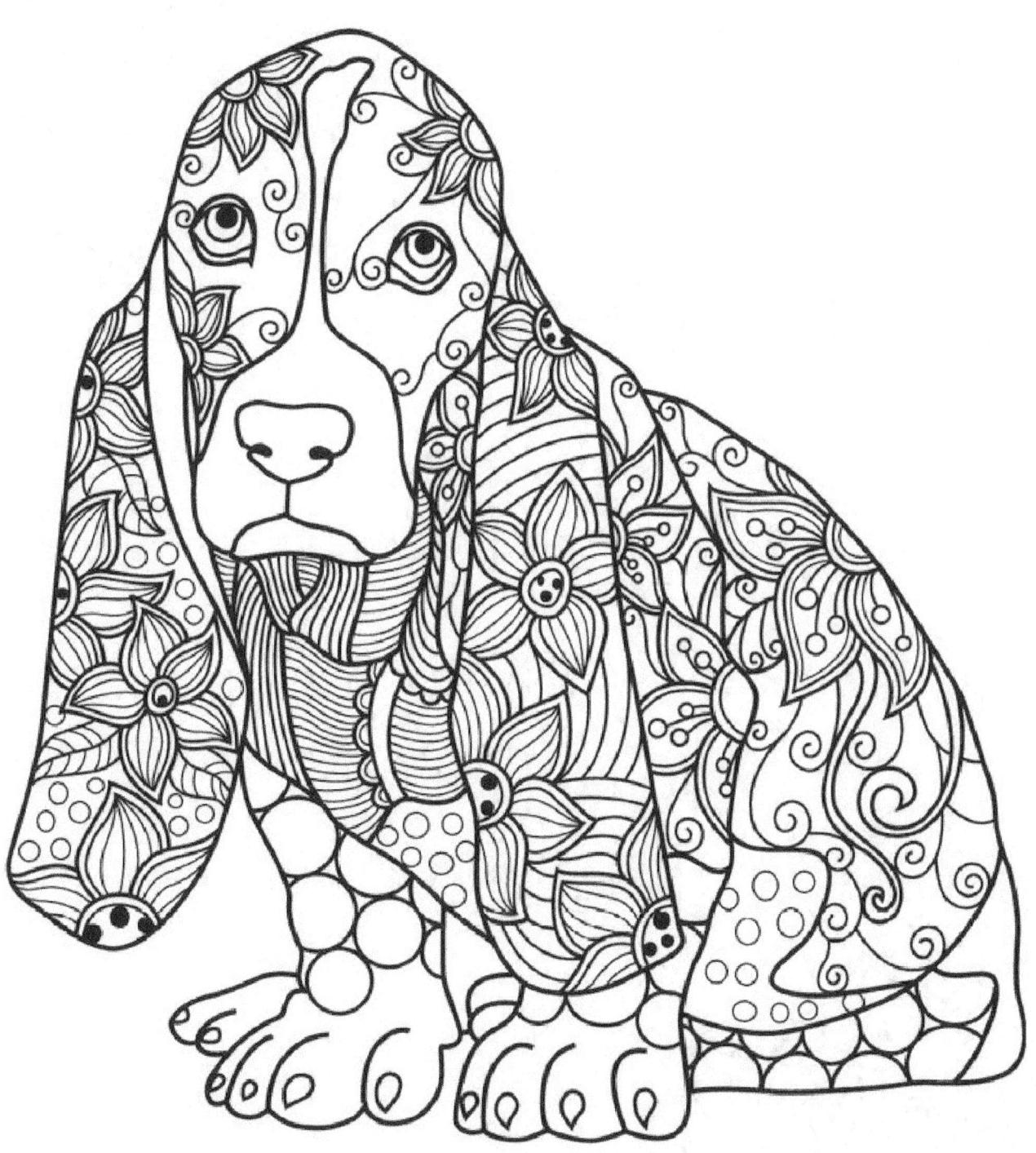

I WILL NOT
COMPARE
MYSELF TO
STRANGERS
ON THE
INTERNET

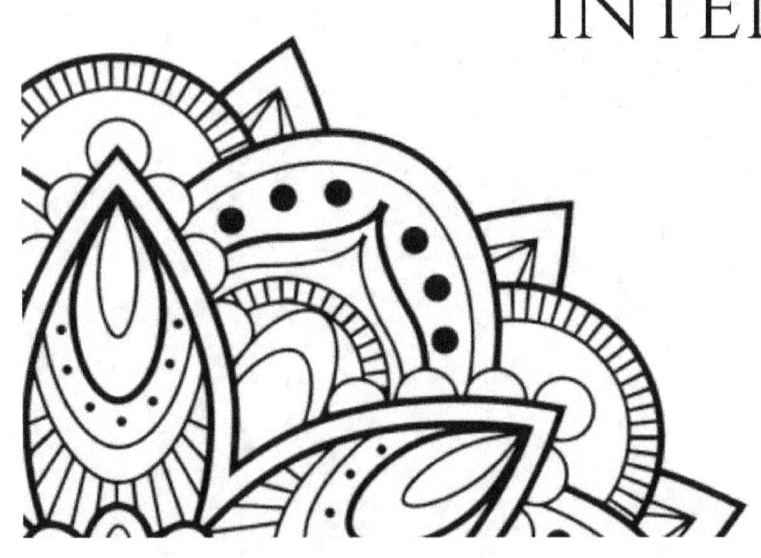

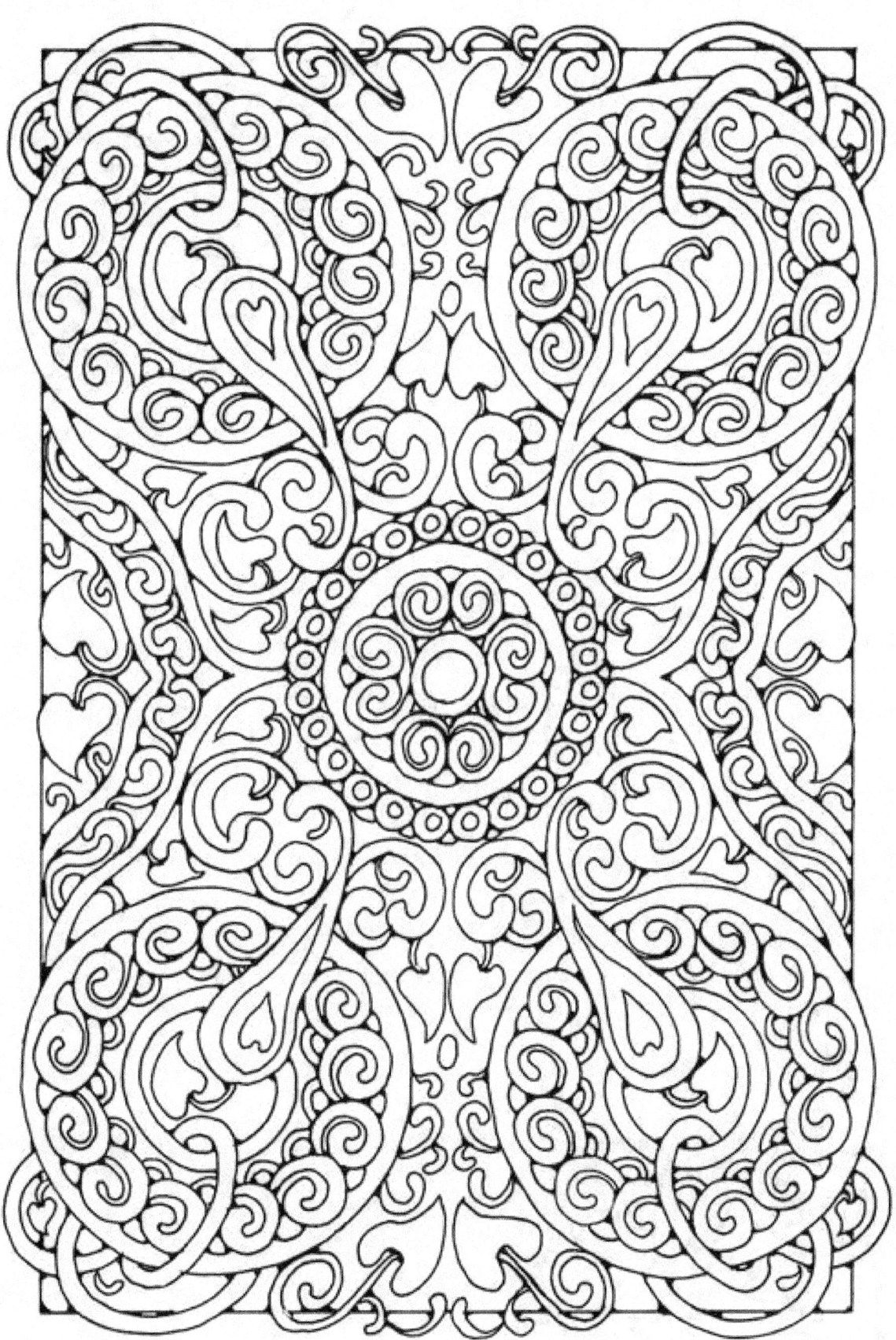

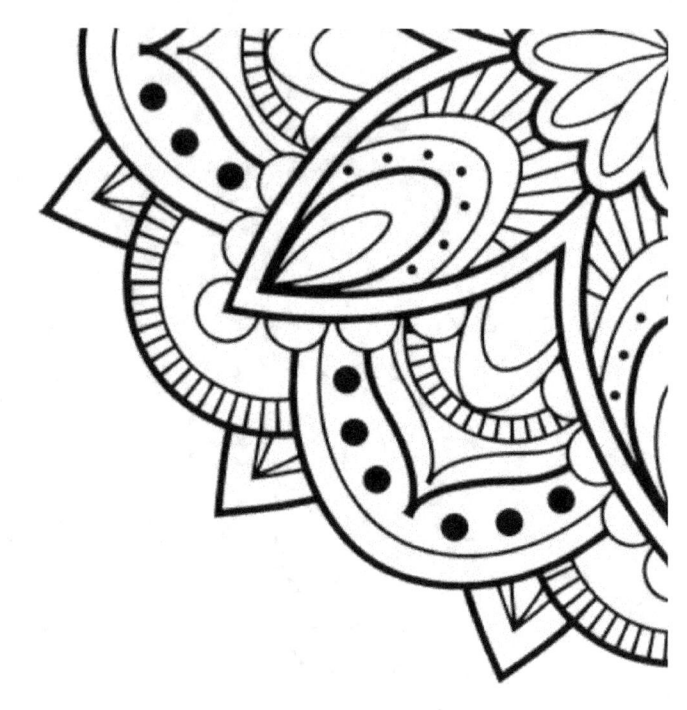

I AM ENOUGH

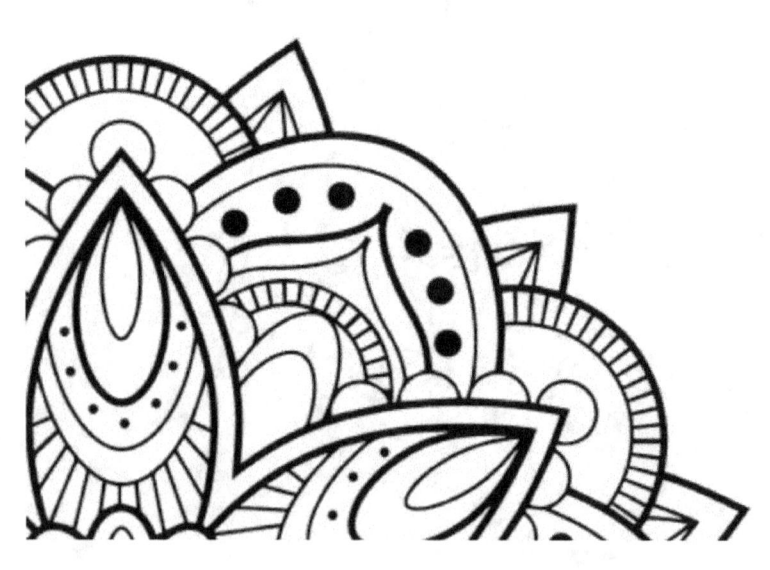

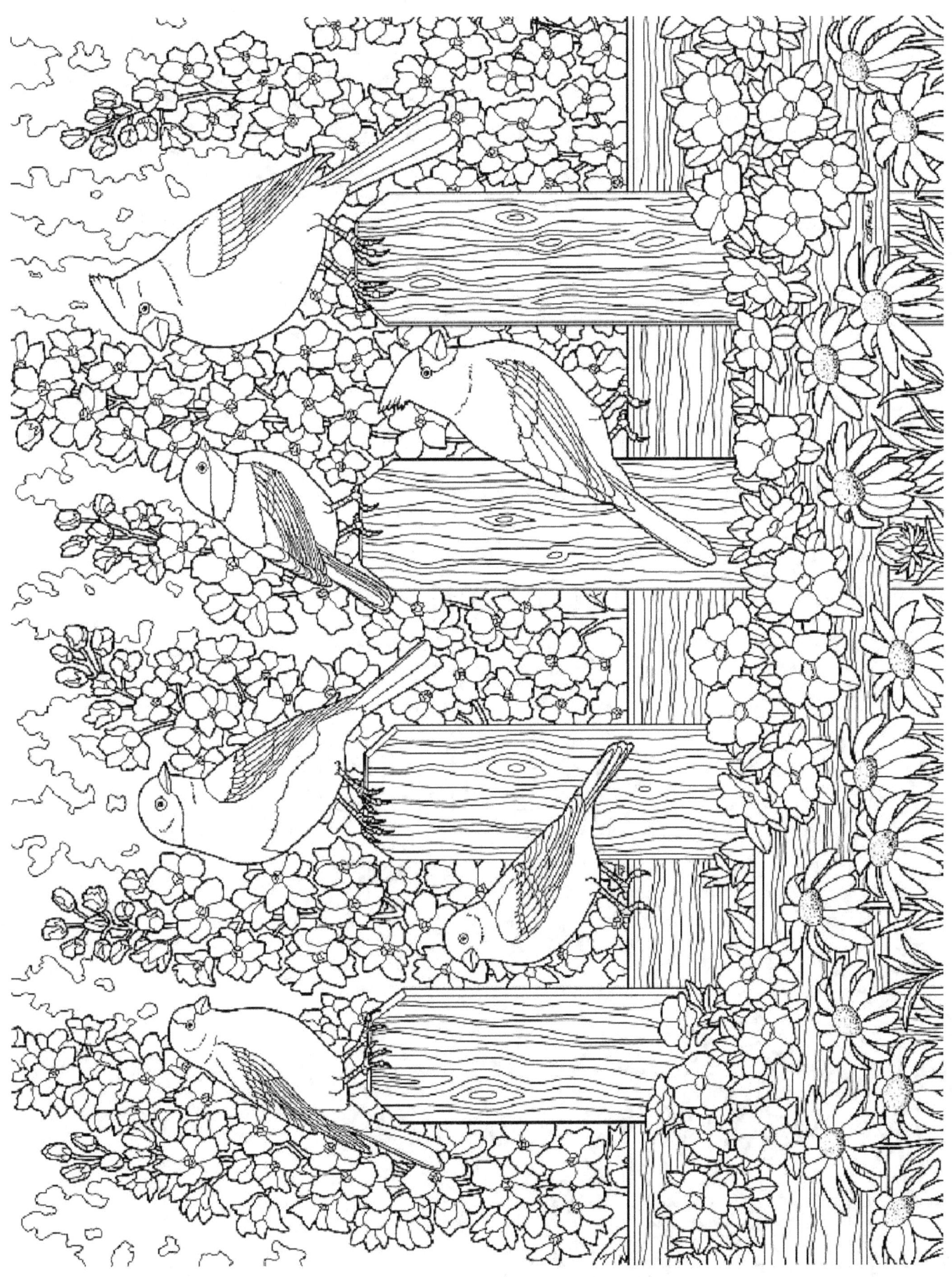

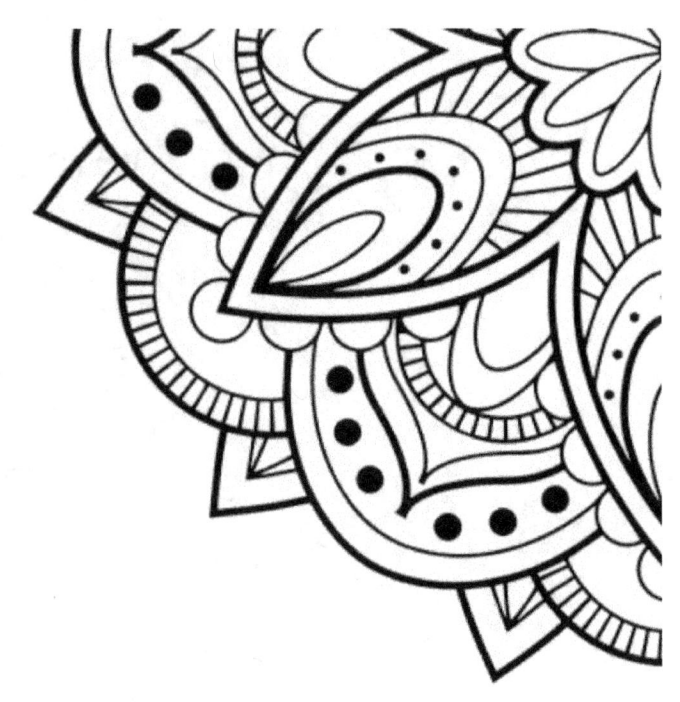

I LET GO
OF ALL
THAT
NO LONGER
SERVES ME

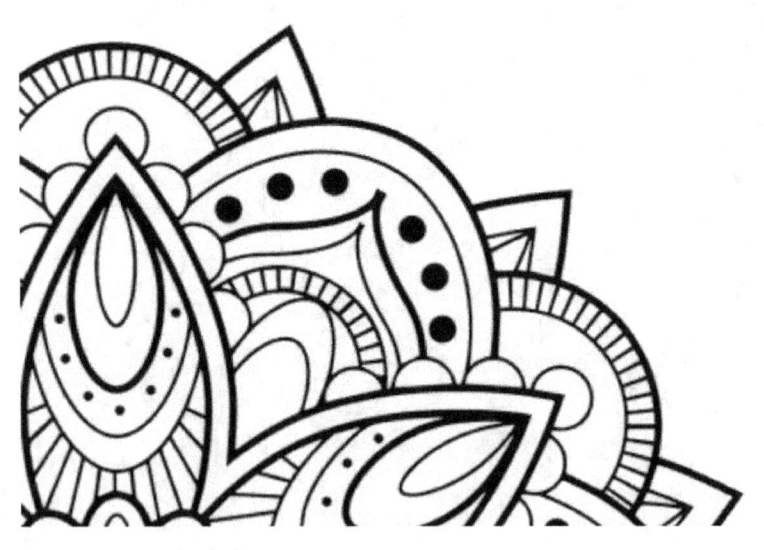

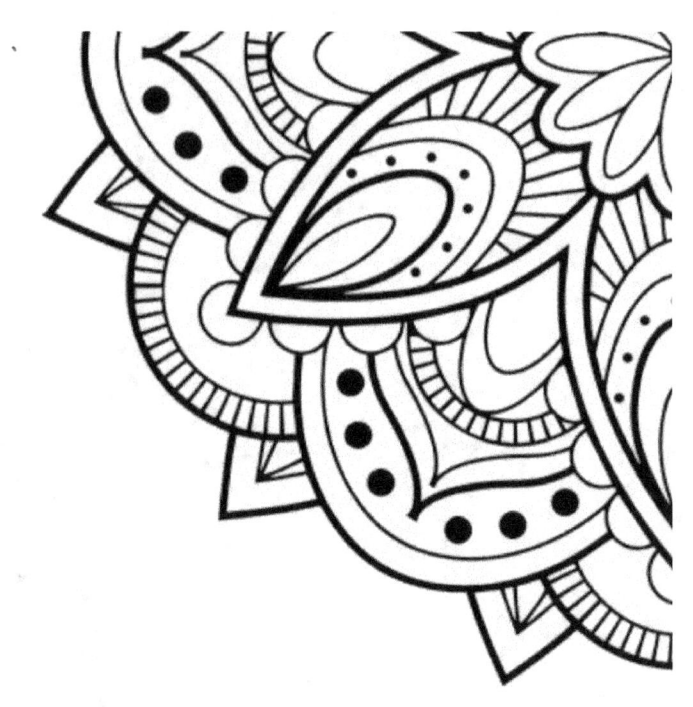

I AM STRONG
AND
CONFIDENT

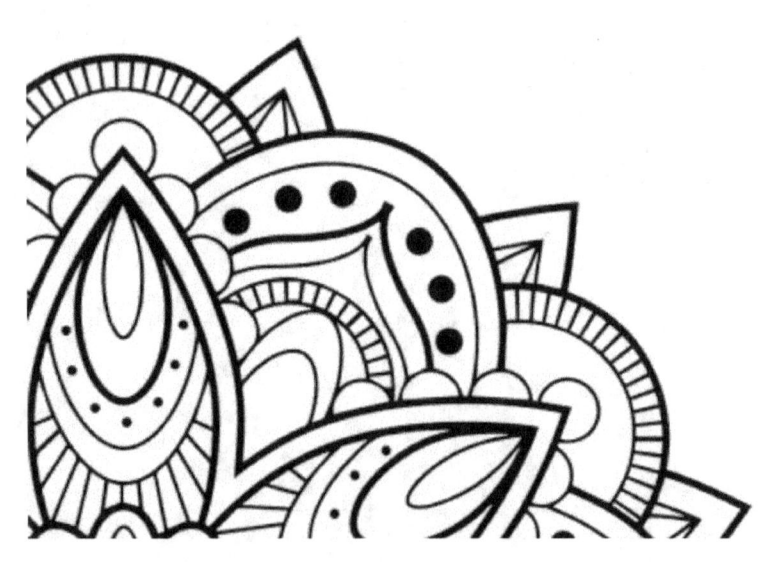

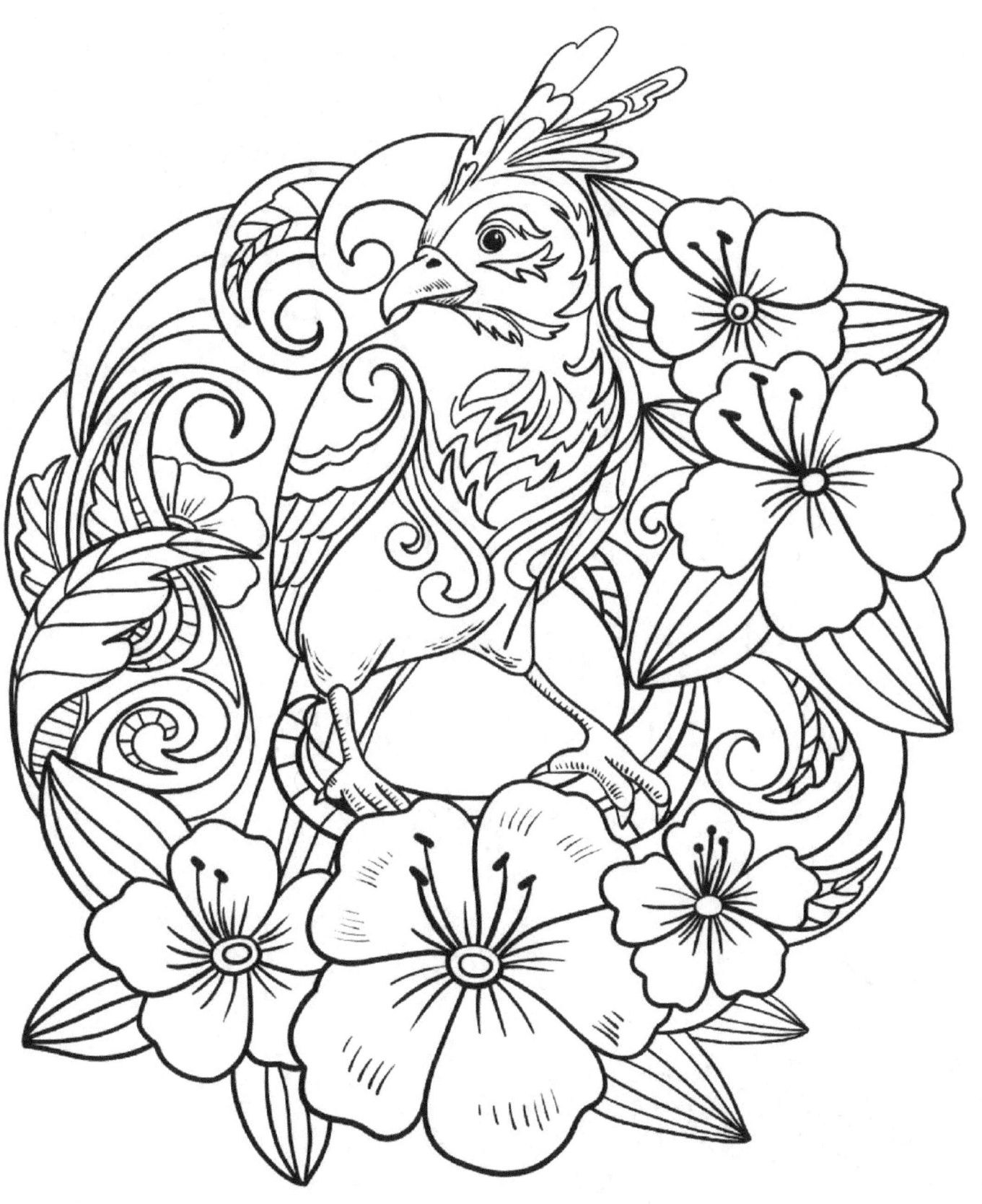

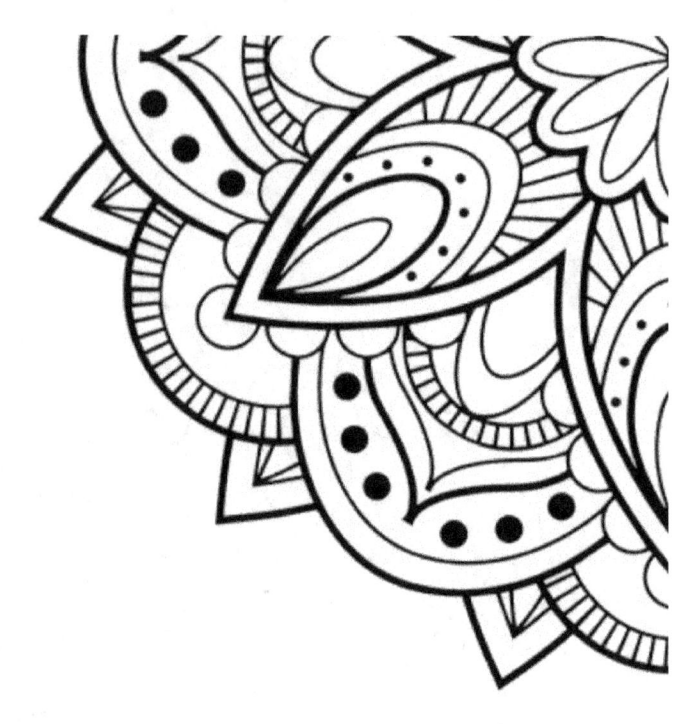

I REFUSE TO GIVE UP BECAUSE I HAVEN'T TRIED ALL POSSIBLE WAYS

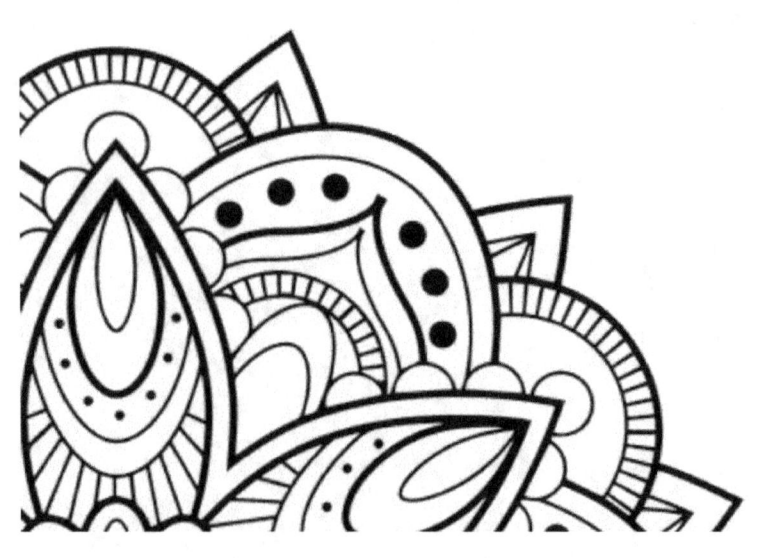

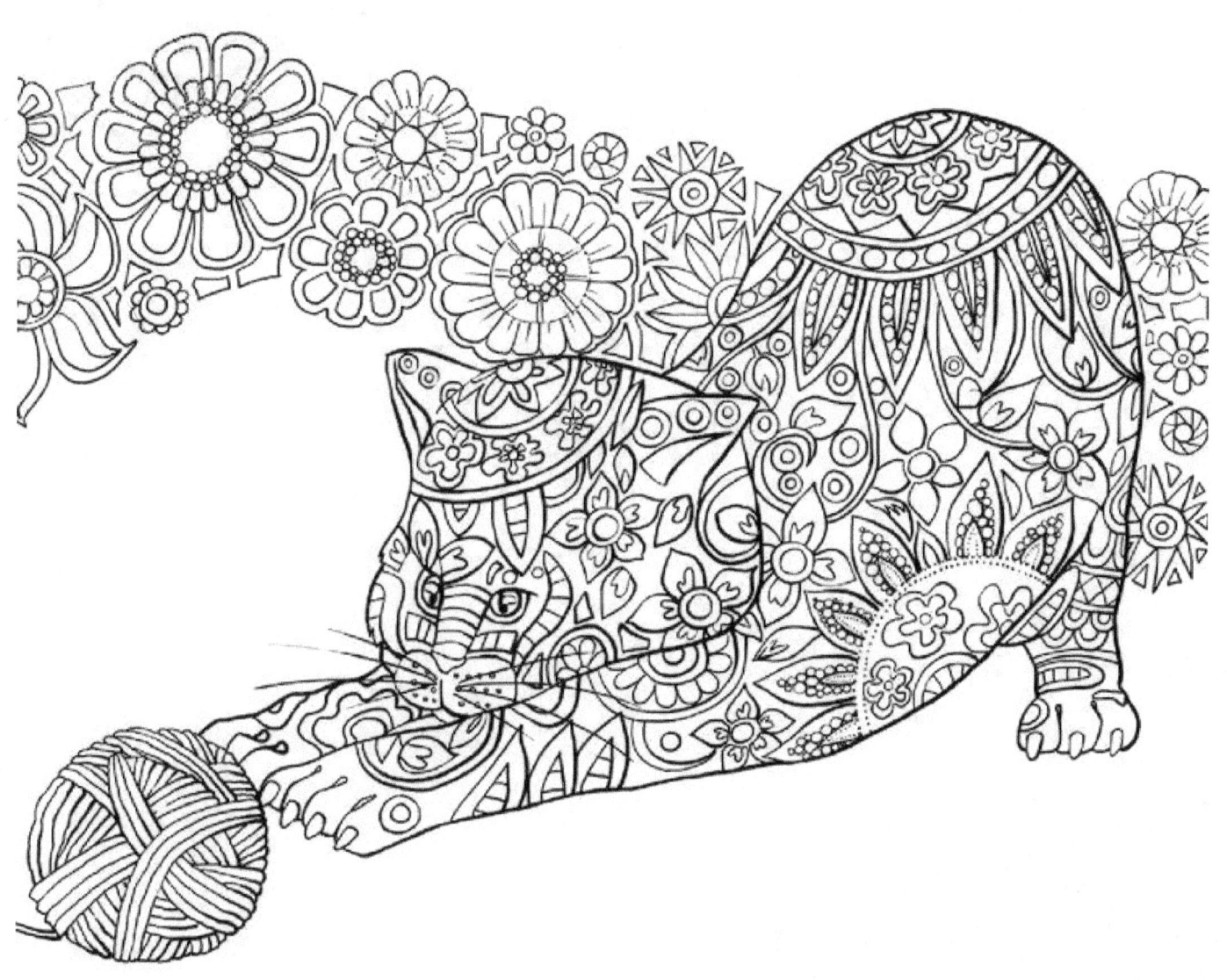

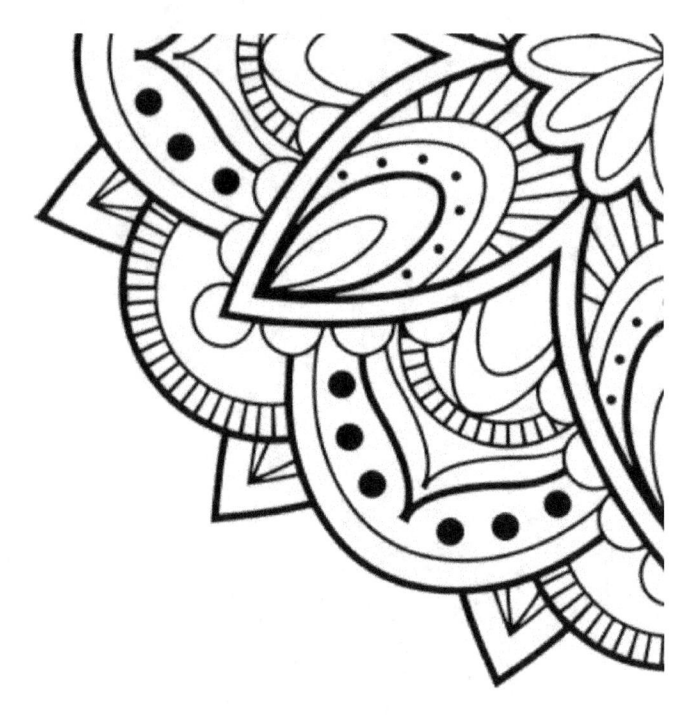

I RELEASE ALL FEAR

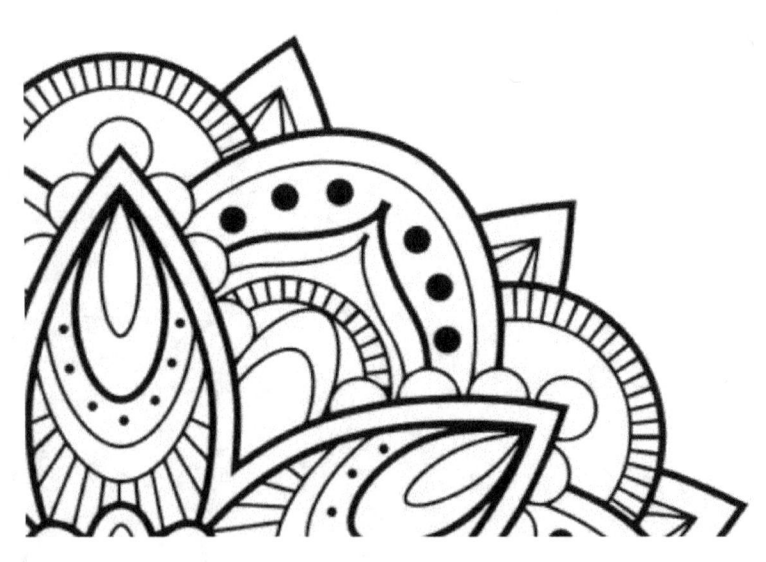

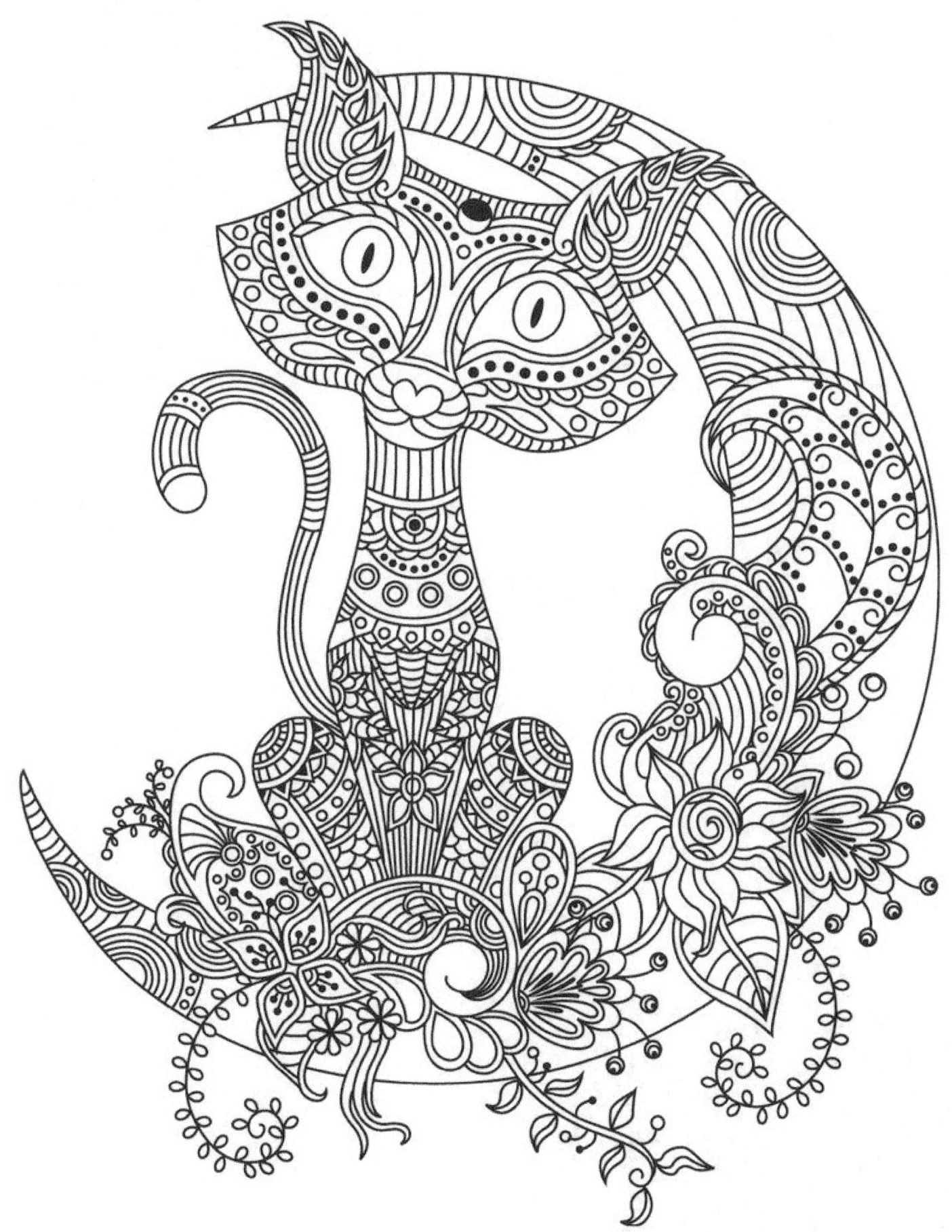

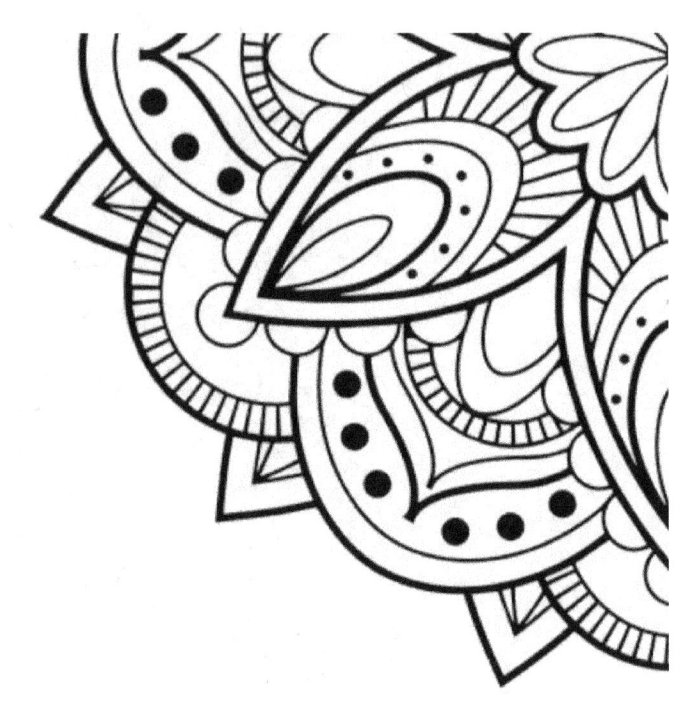

MY PRESENCE IS
MY POWER

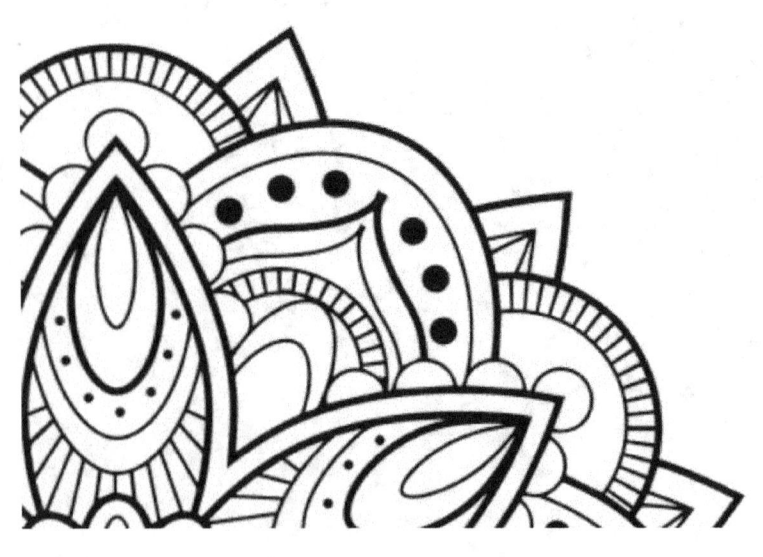

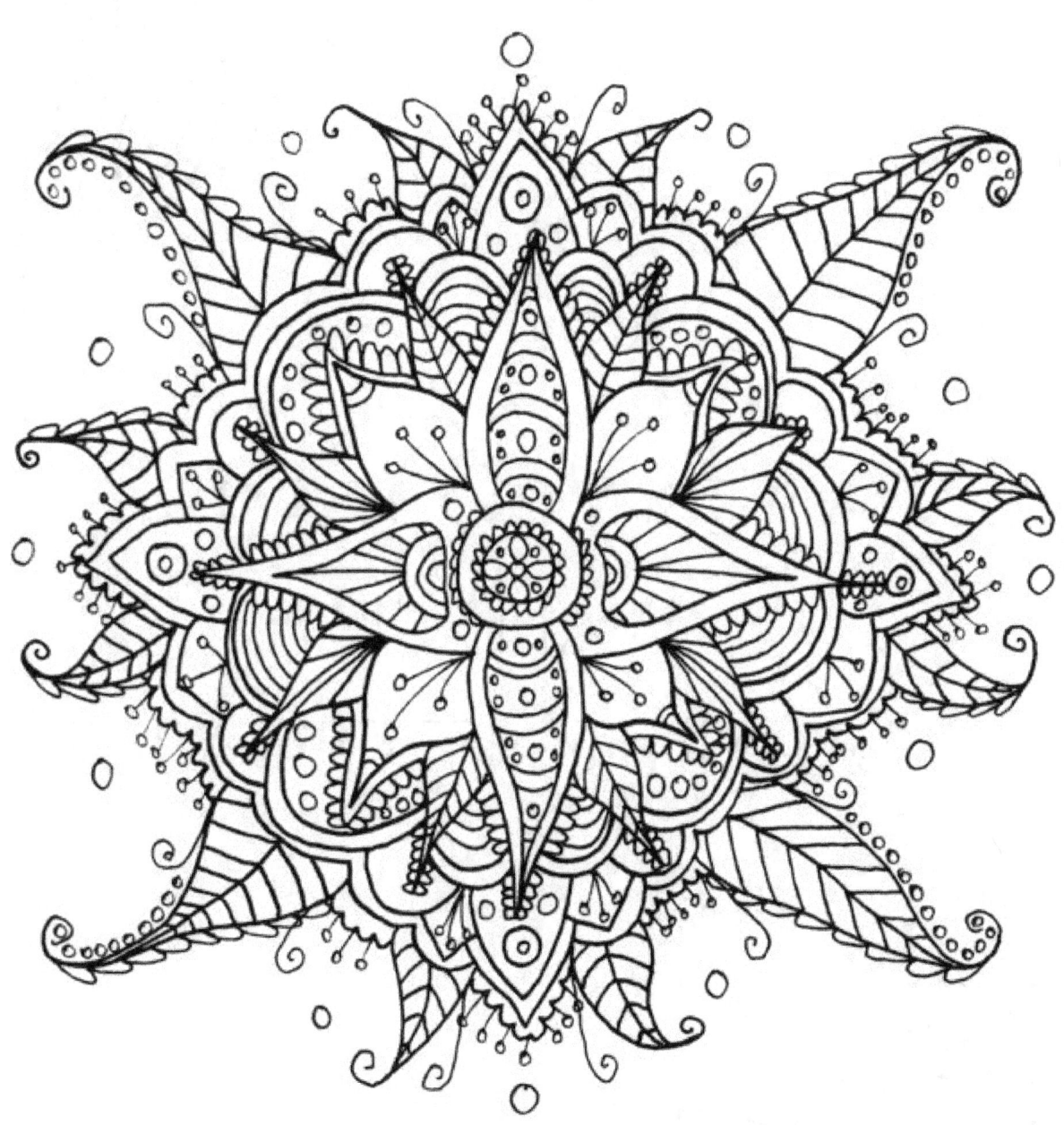

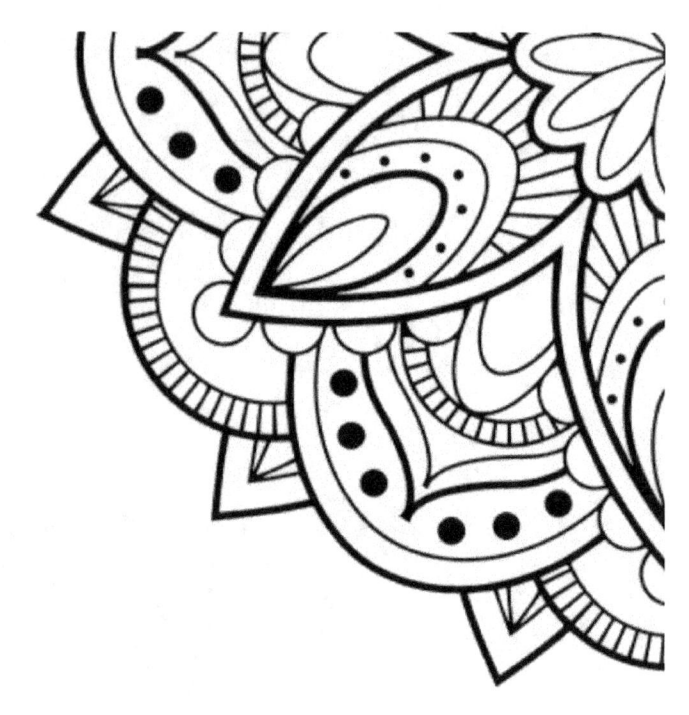

WHEN YOU REALLY
WANT IT,
YOU ARE UNSTOPPABLE

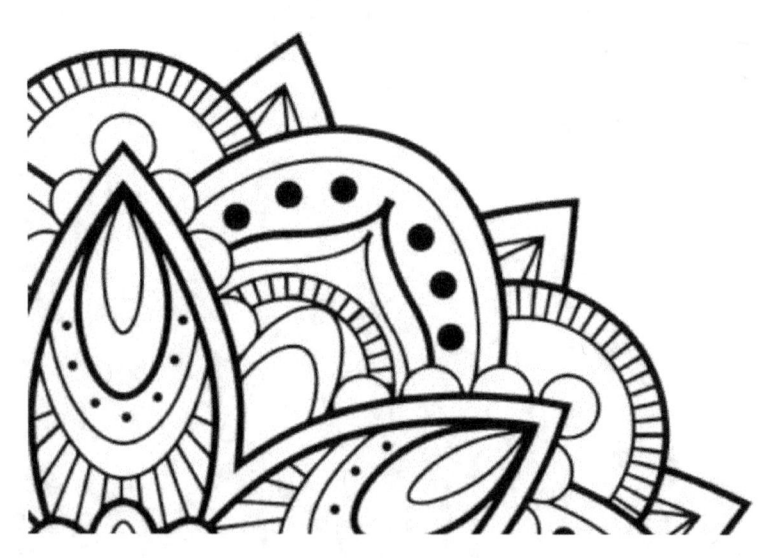

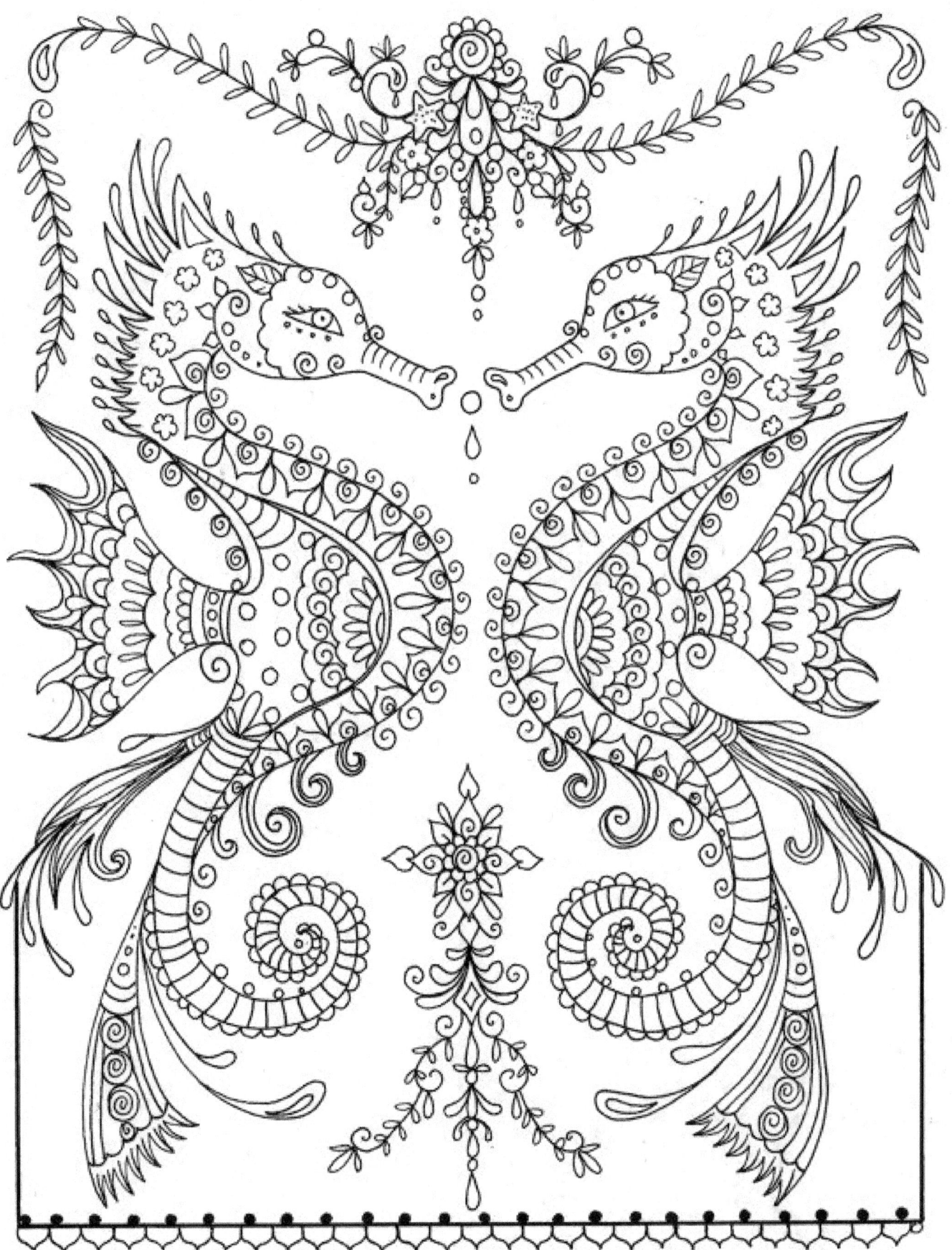

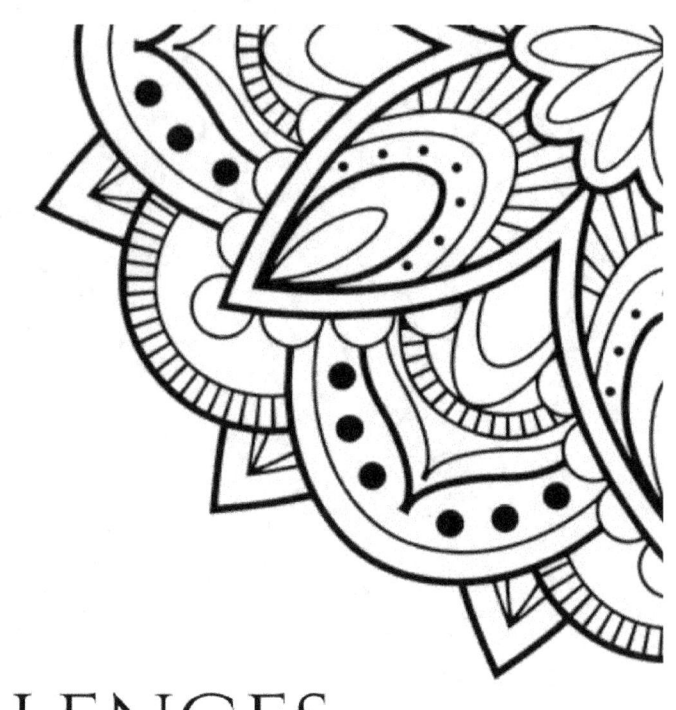

I SEE CHALLENGES
WHERE OTHERS
SEE
DIFFICULTIES

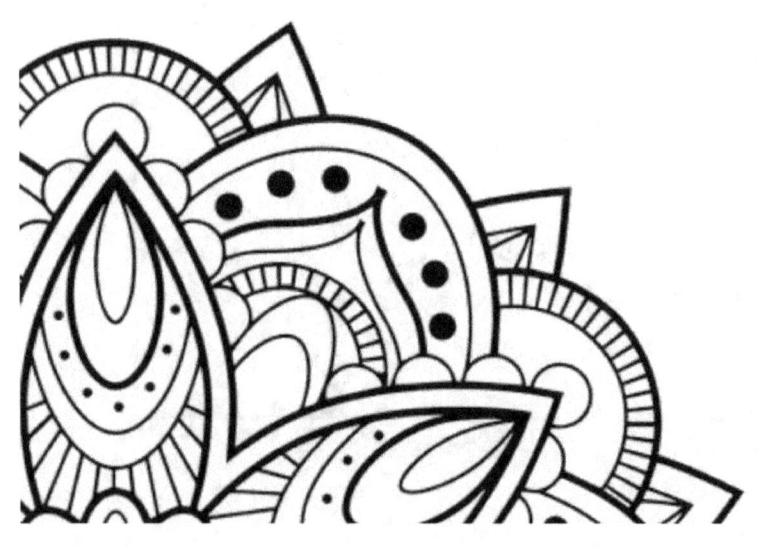

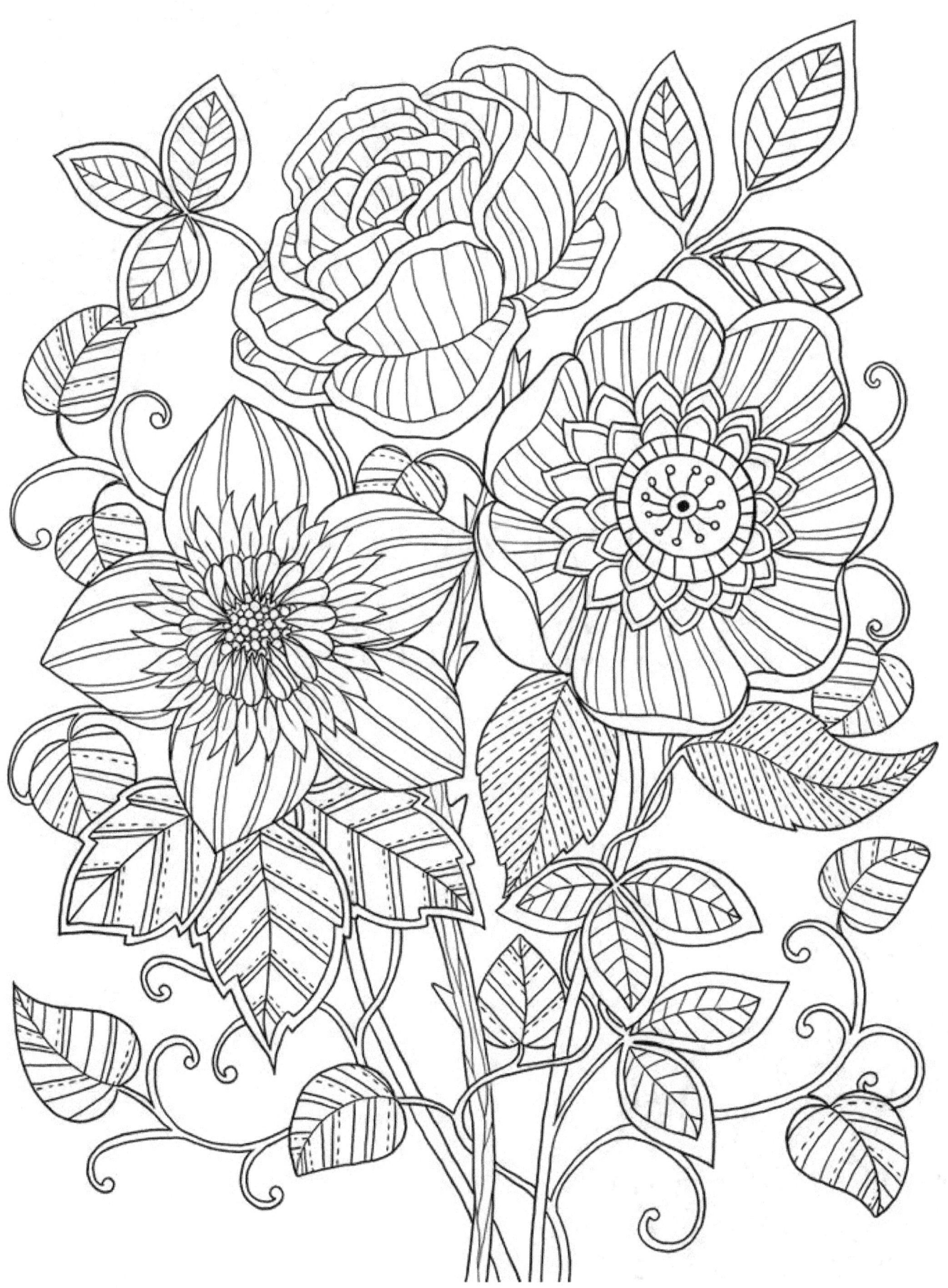

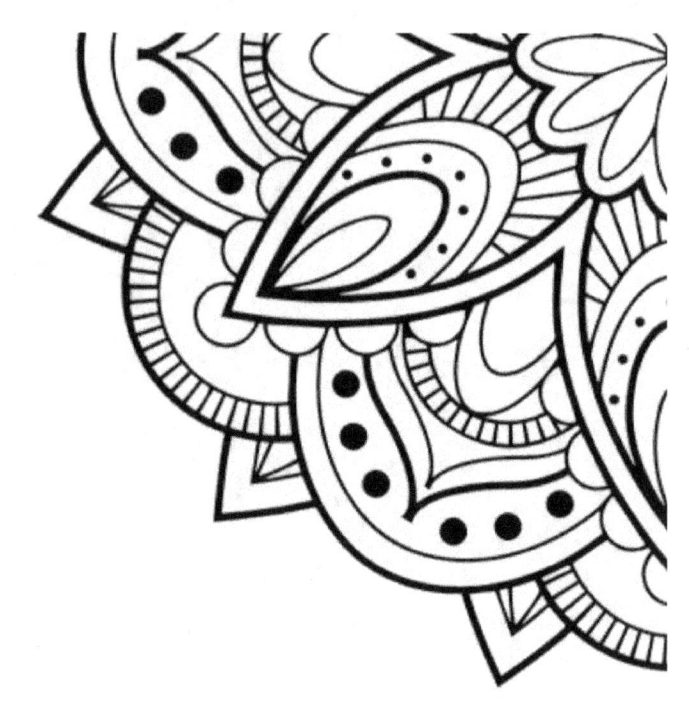

I EMBRACE

SIMPLICITY

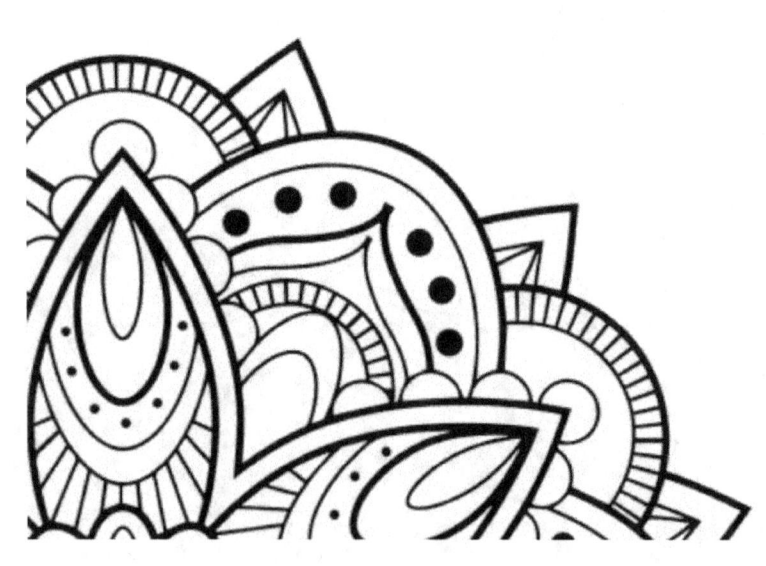

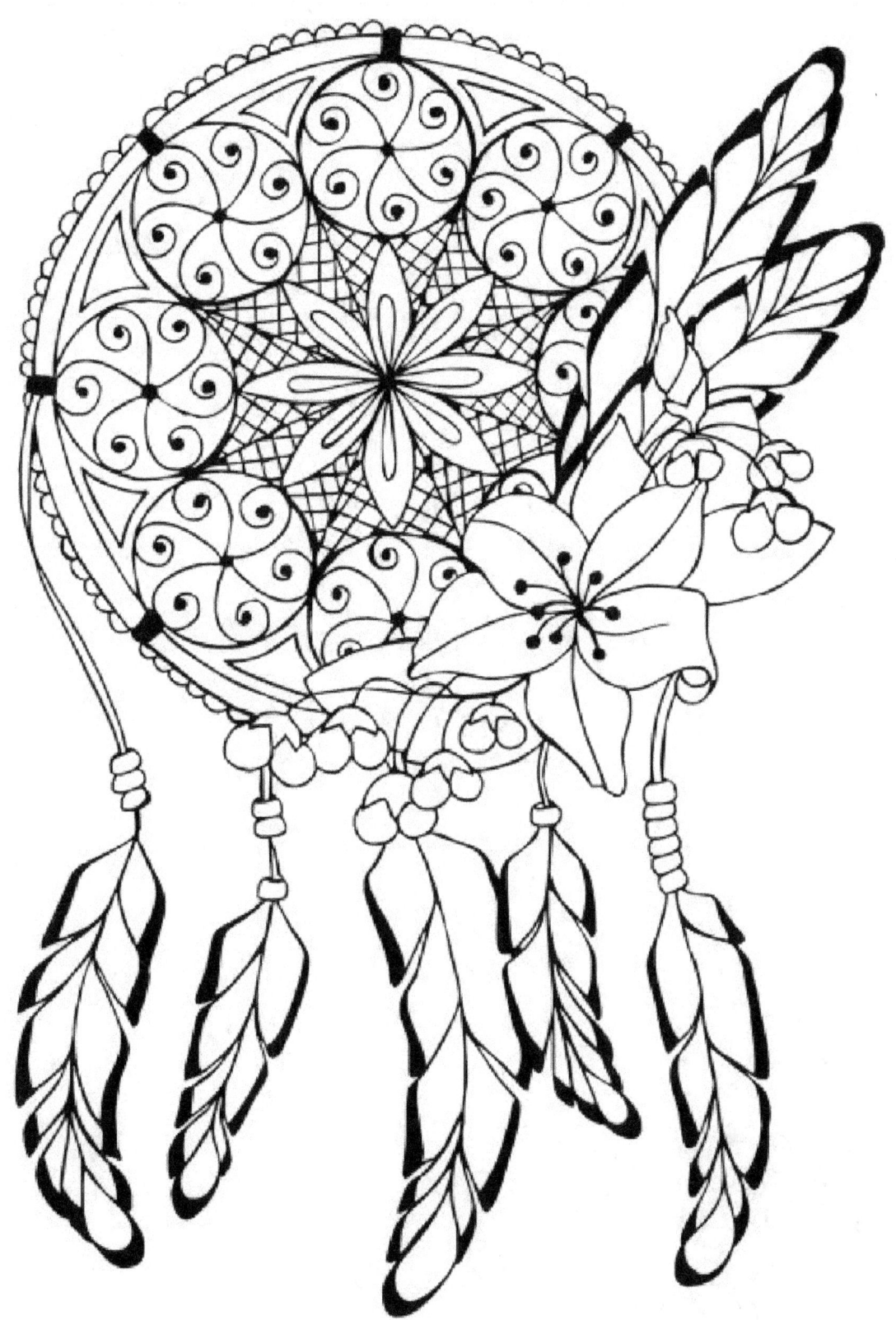

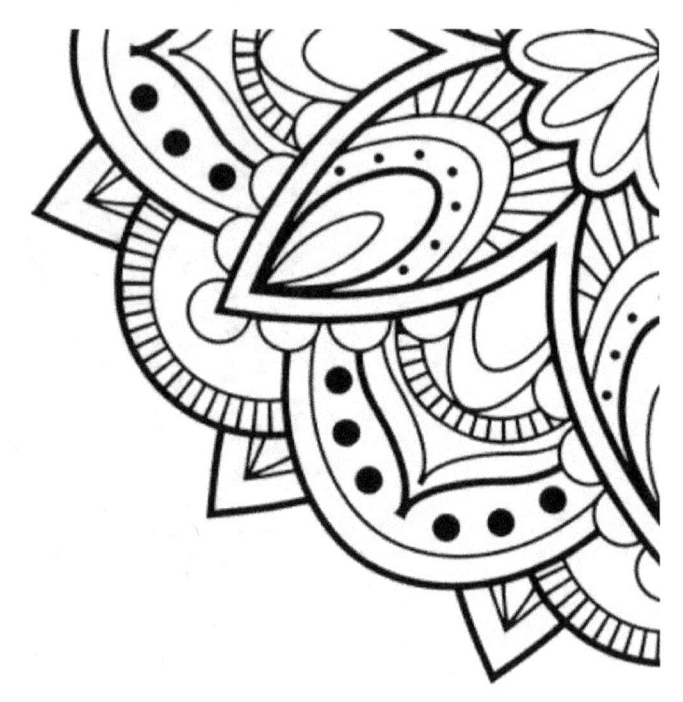

PURSUE

YOUR

DREAMS

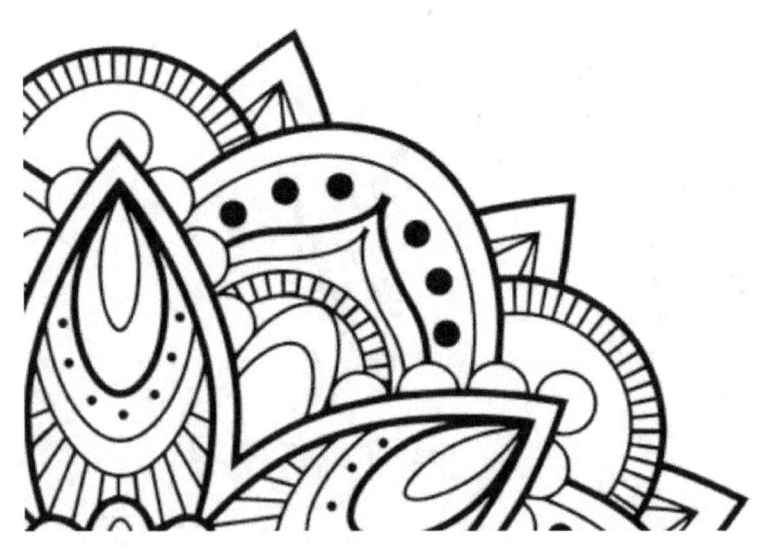

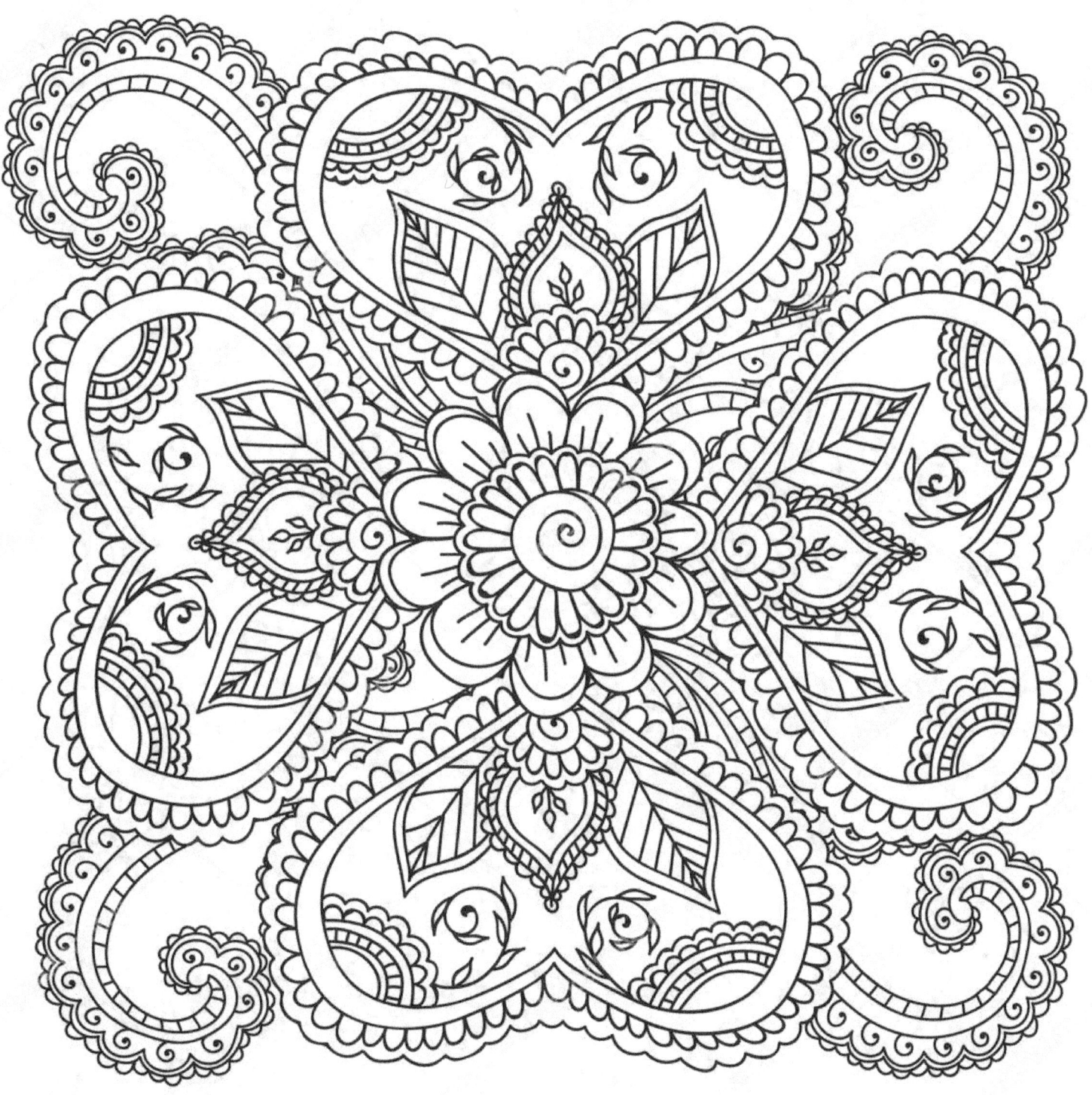

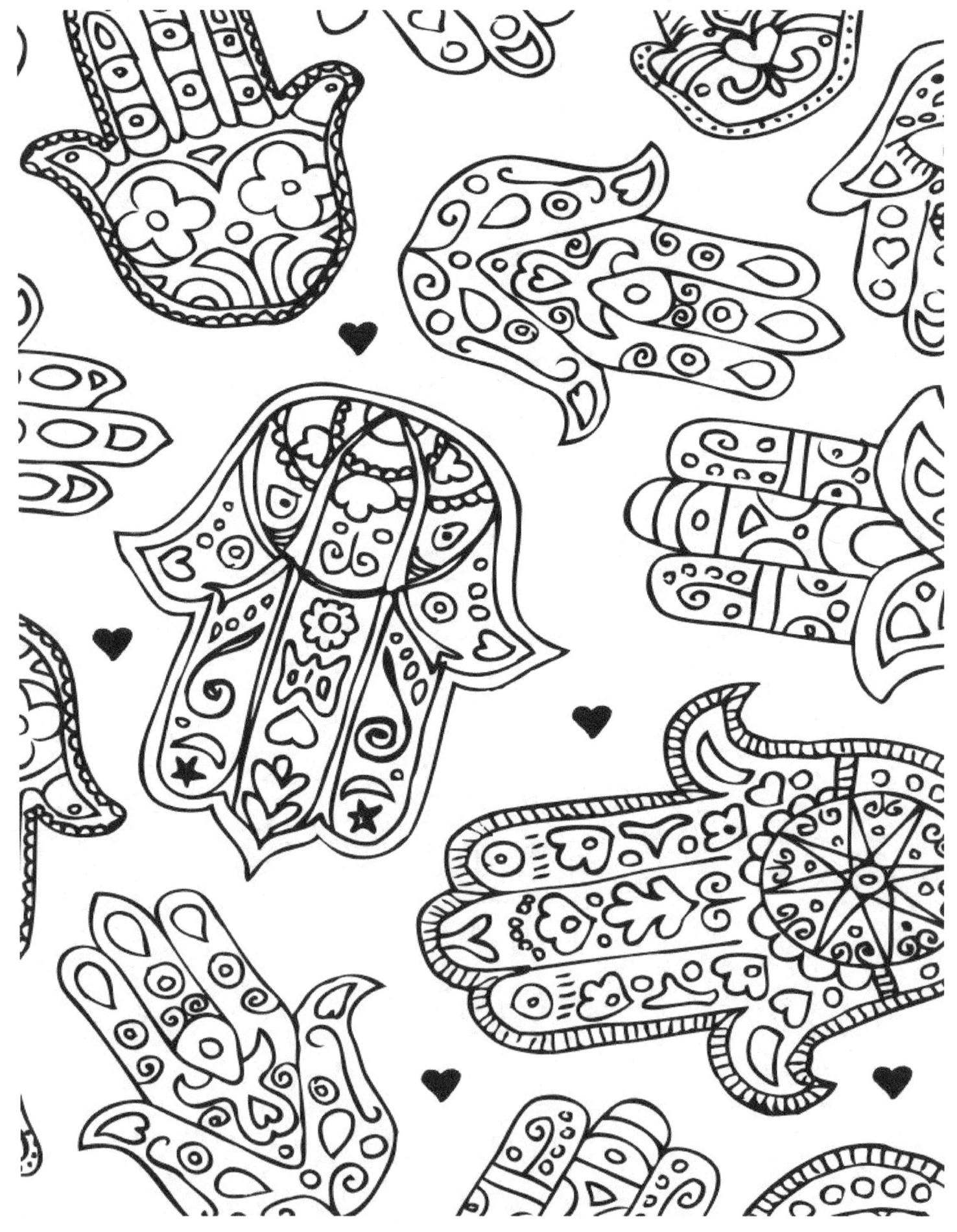

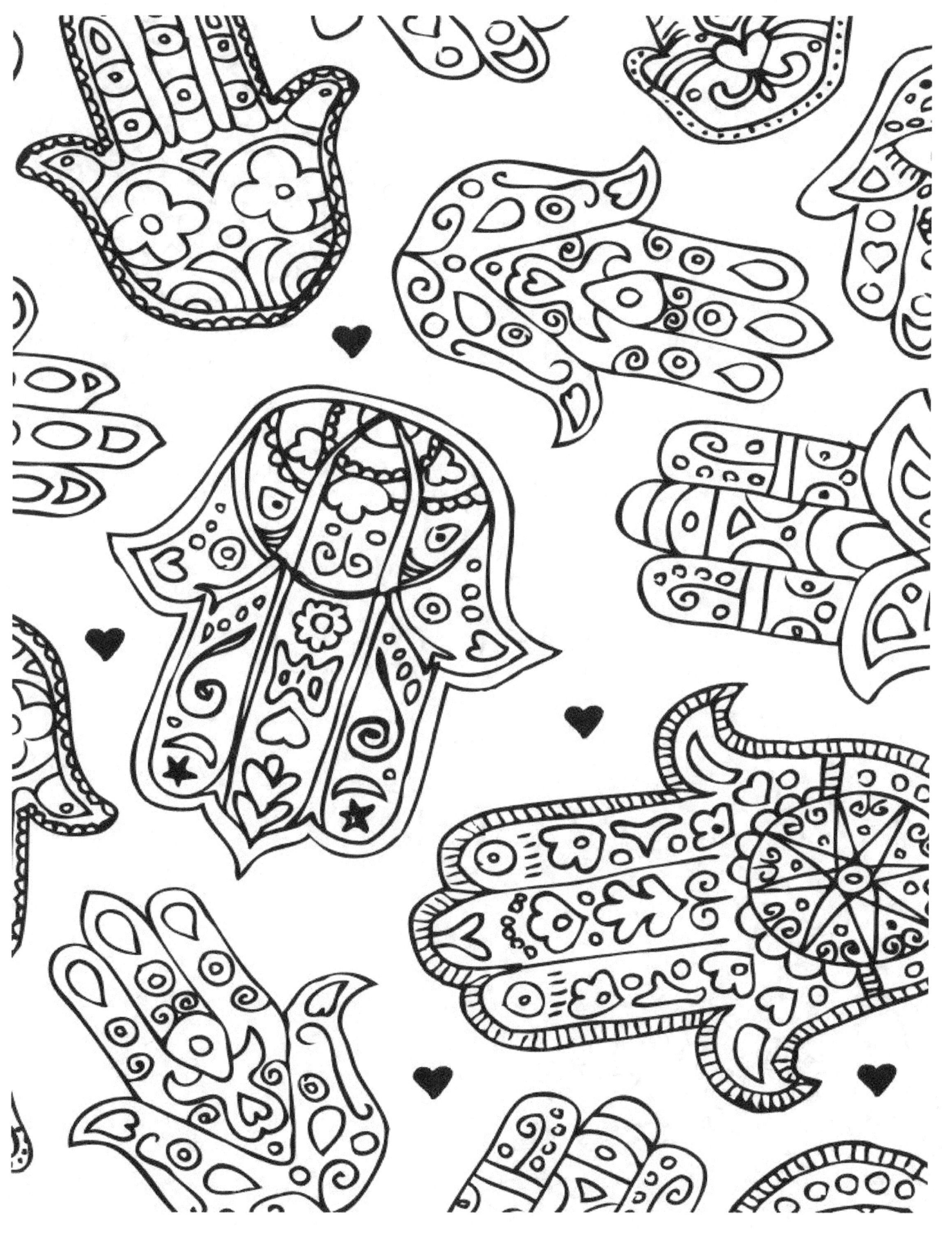

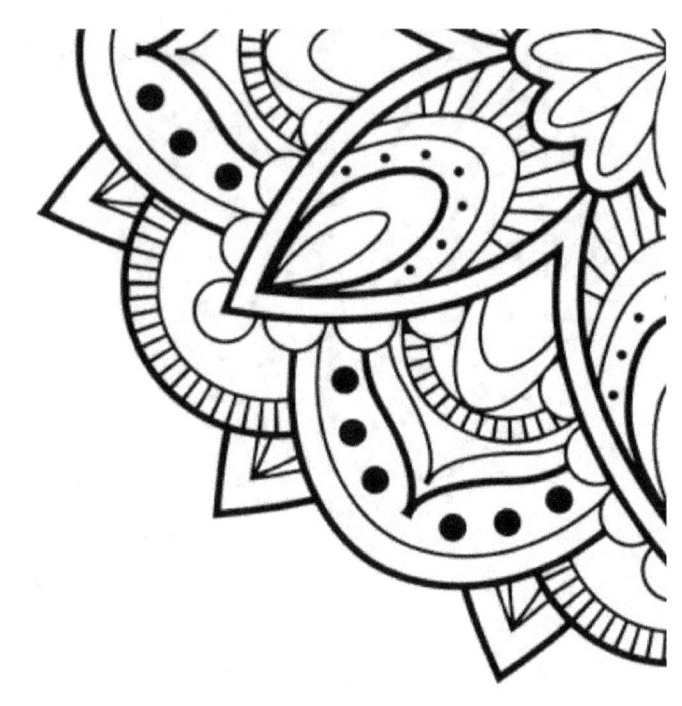

ALL YOUR ACTIONS
LEAD TO
ABUNDANCE
&
PROSPERITY

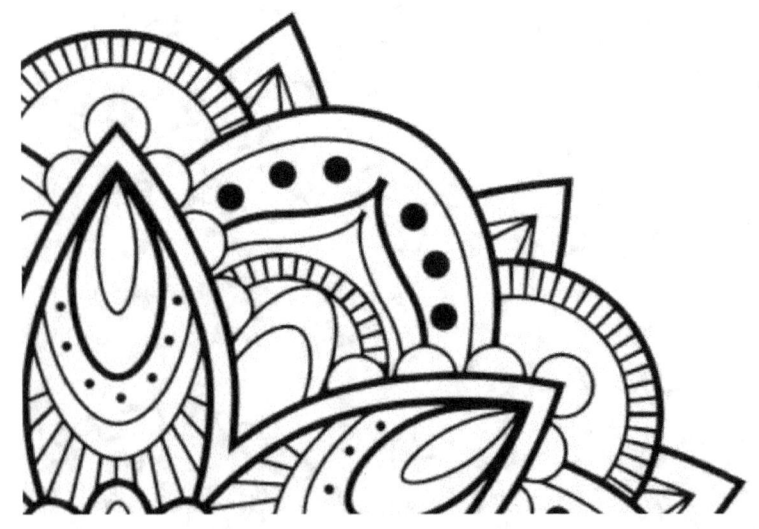

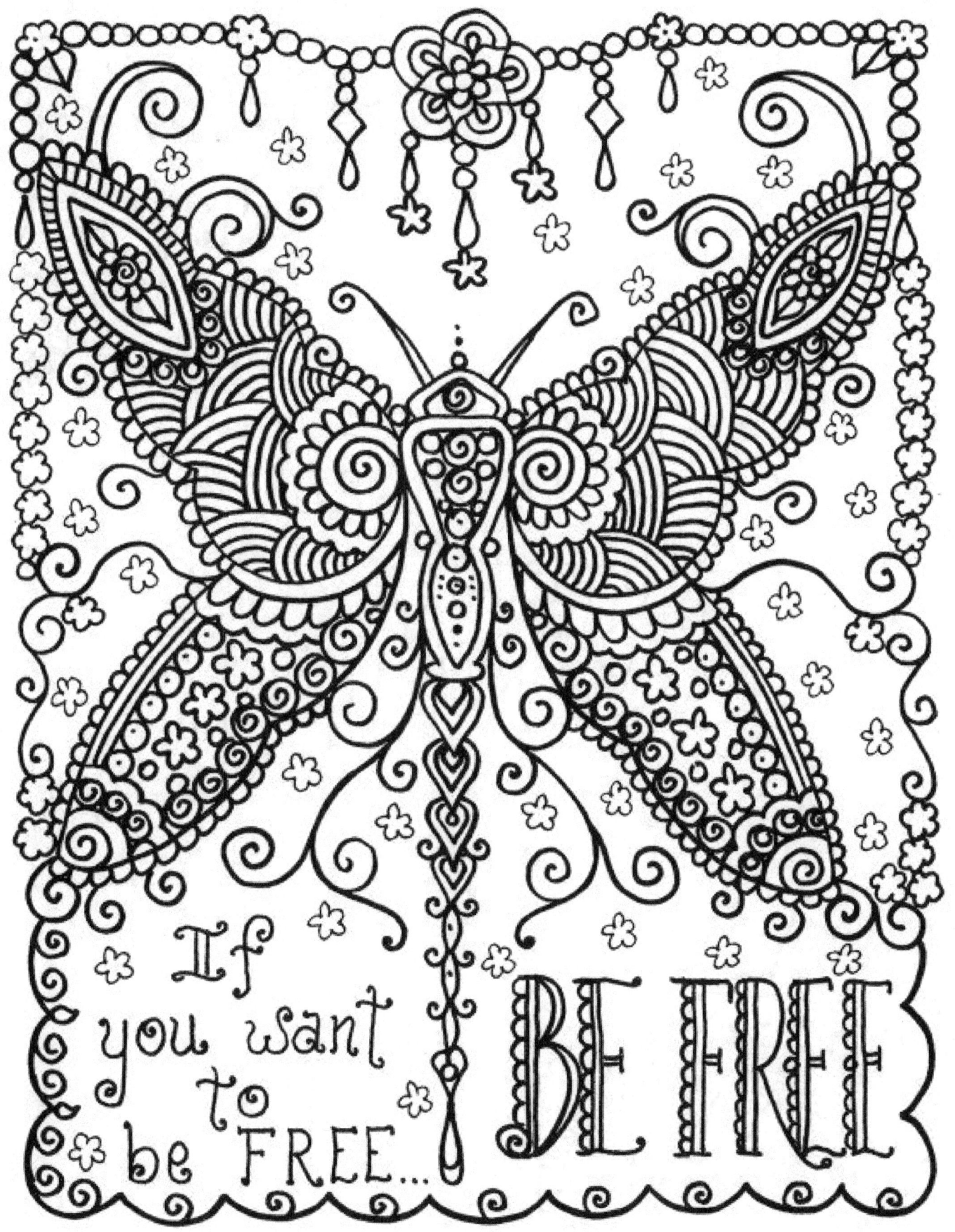

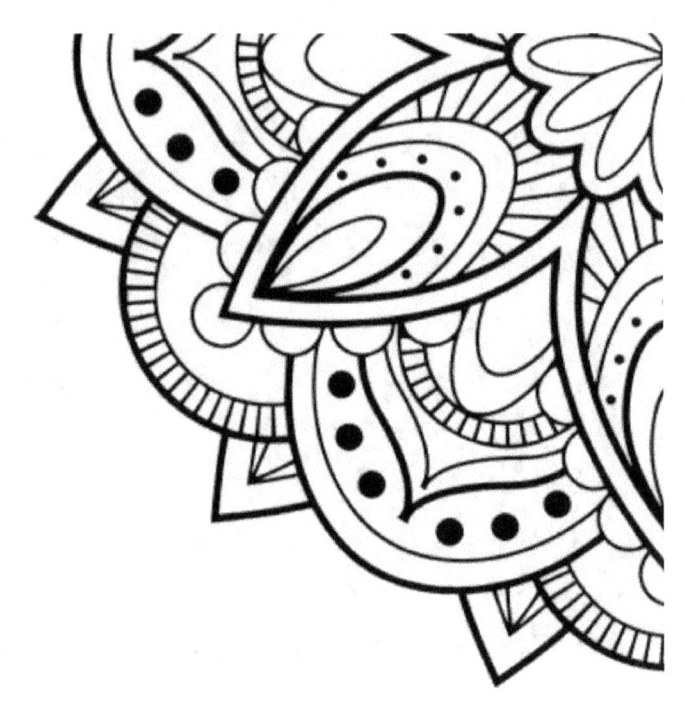

YES, IT'S HARD
BUT IT'S
WORTH IT

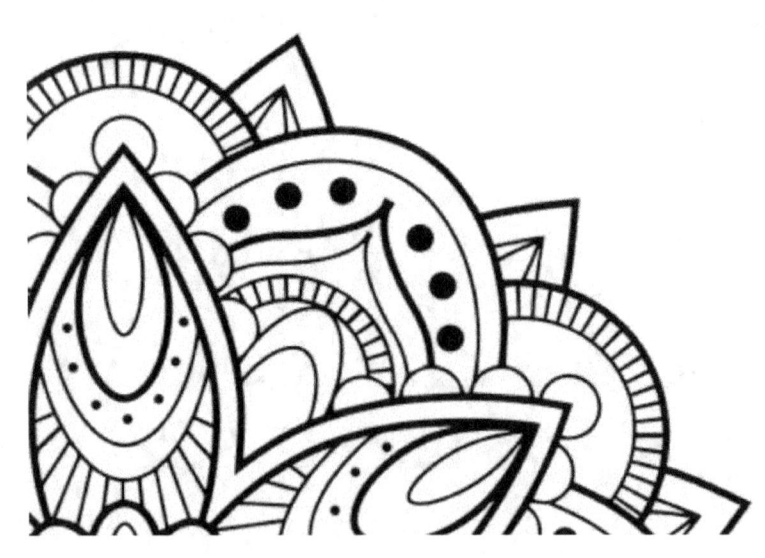

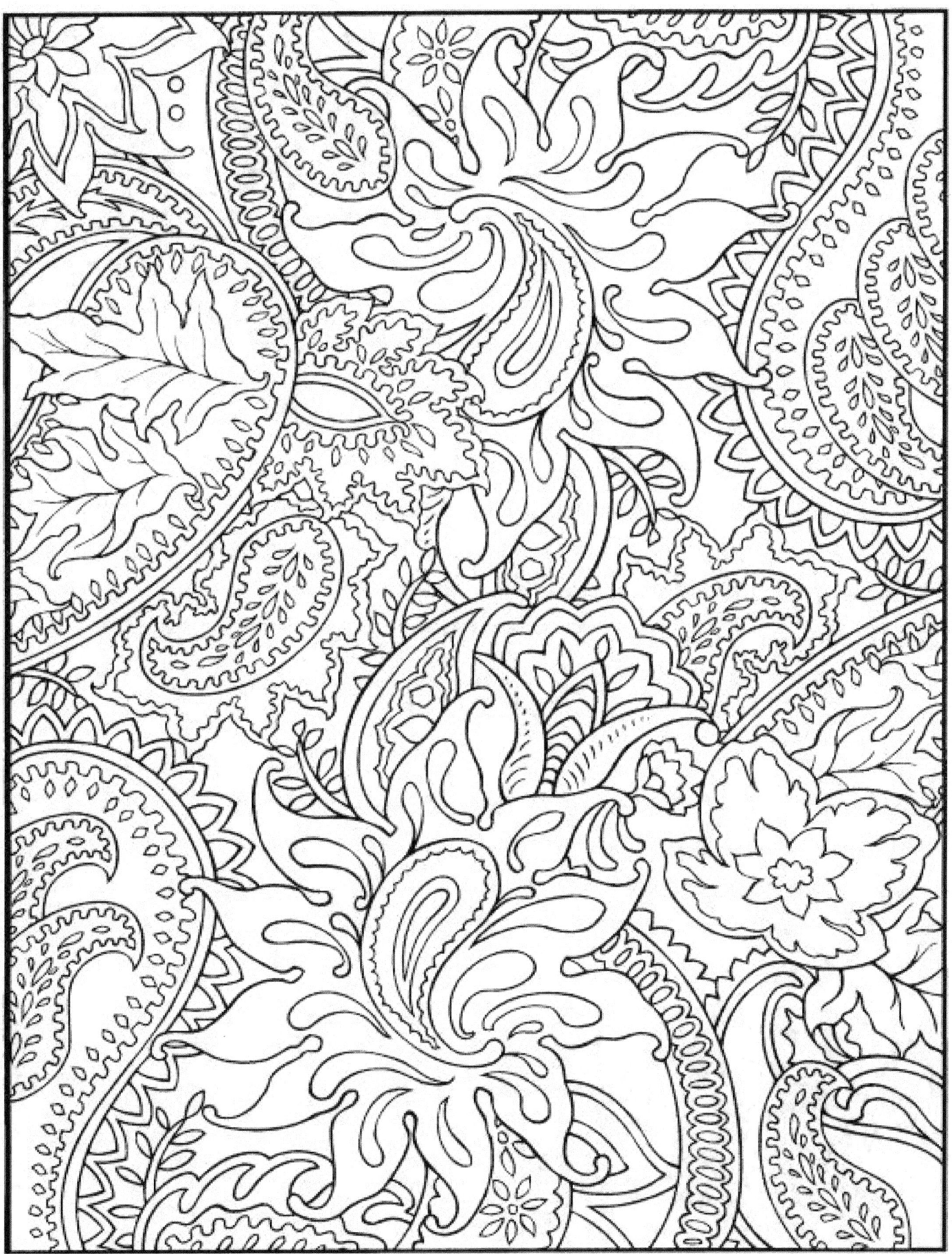

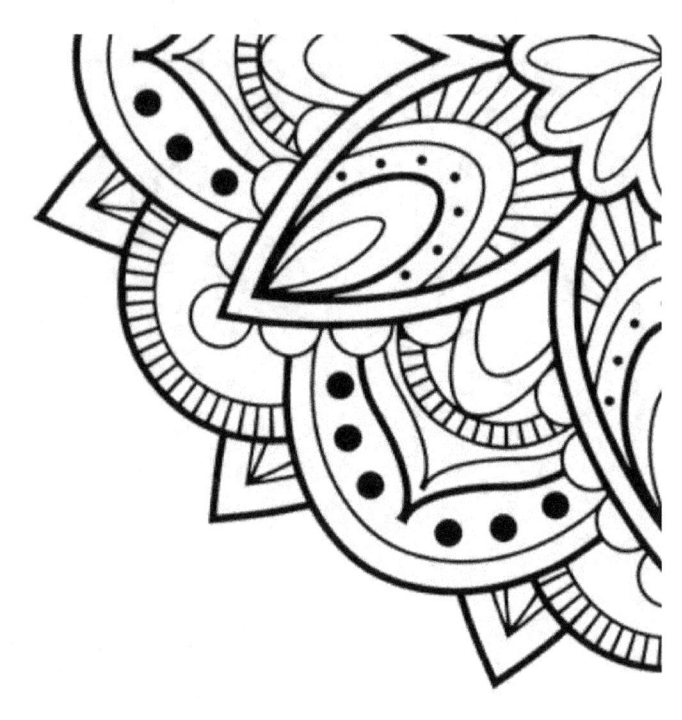

YES, IT'S HARD
BUT IT'S
WORTH IT

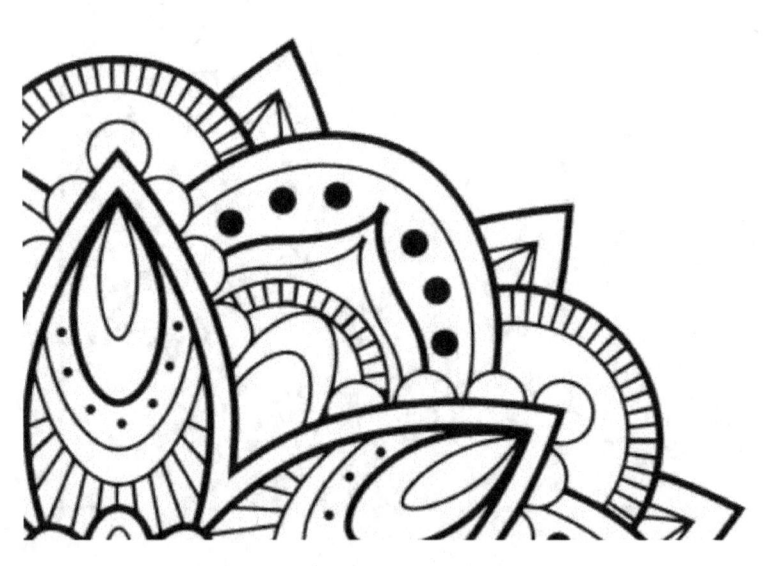

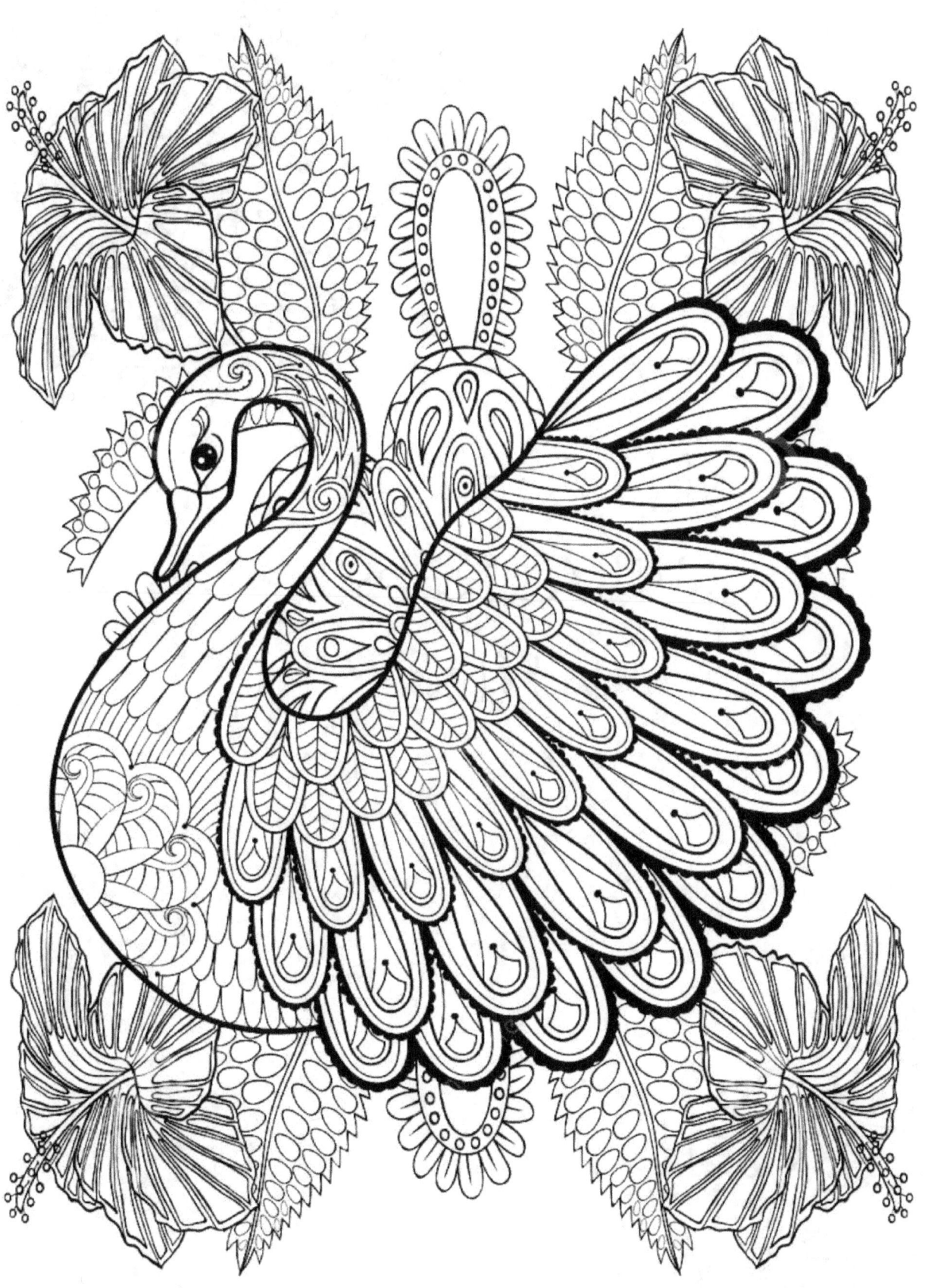

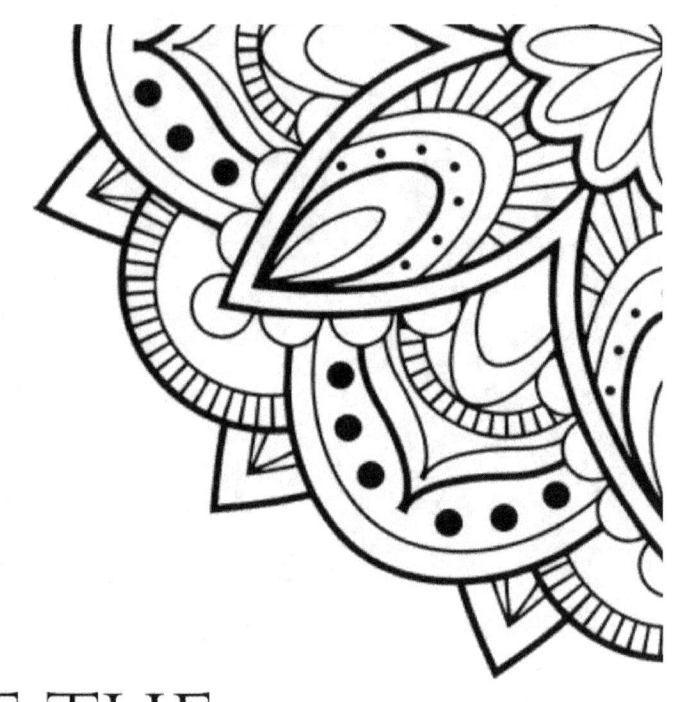

RELEASE THE
GREATNESS
WITHIN
YOU

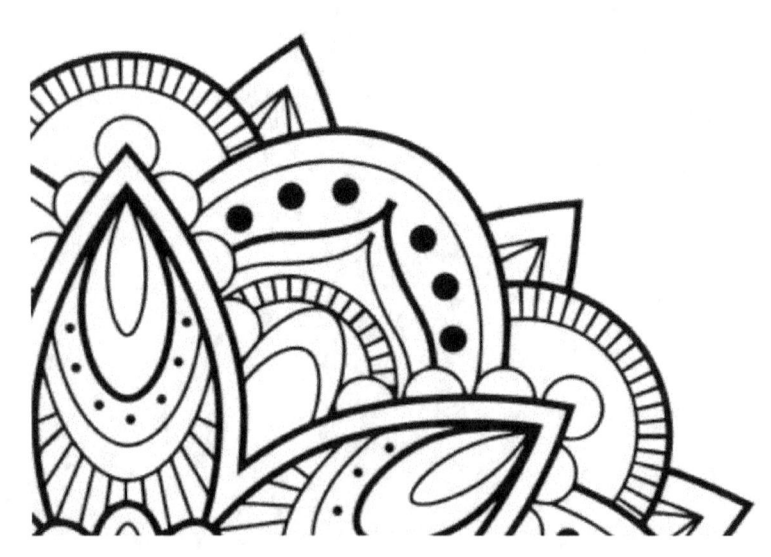

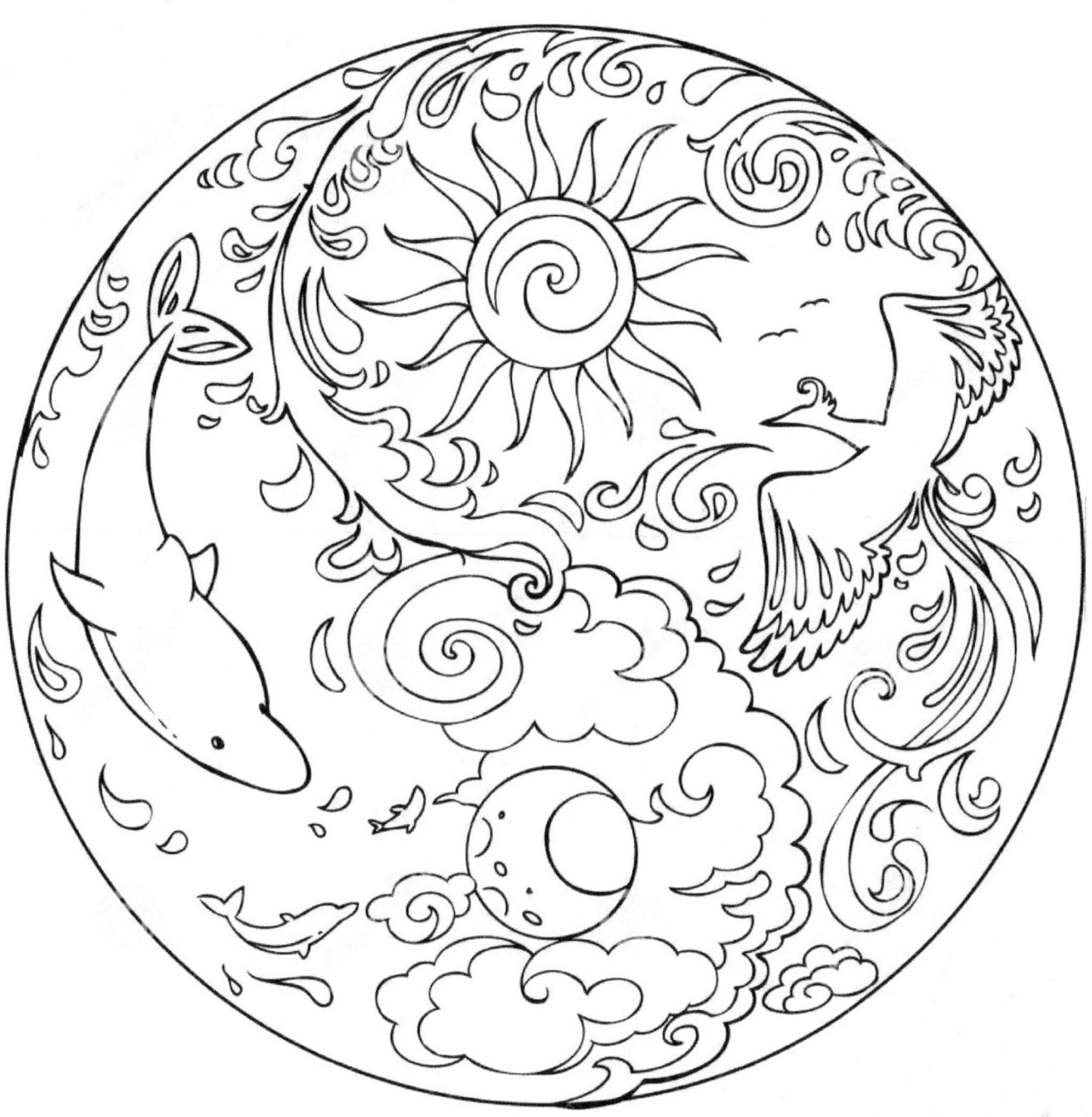

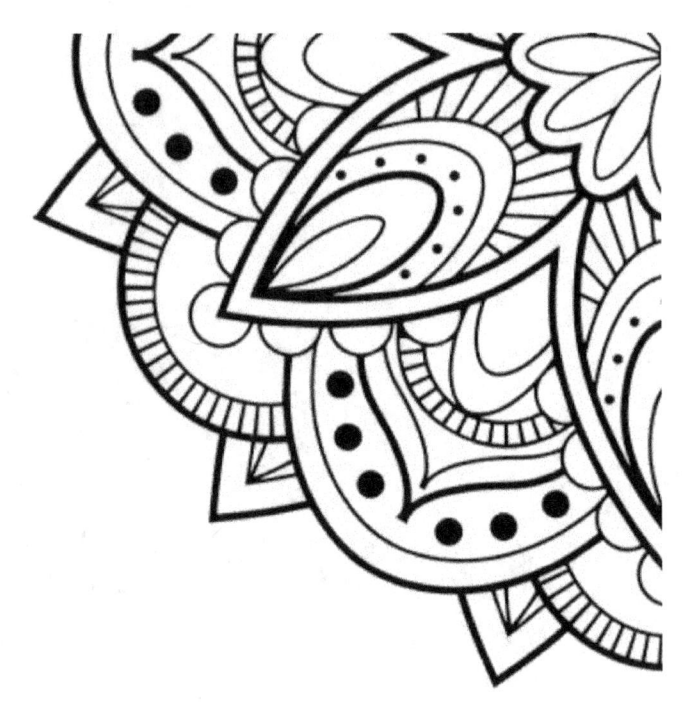

SHOW GRATITUDE DAILY

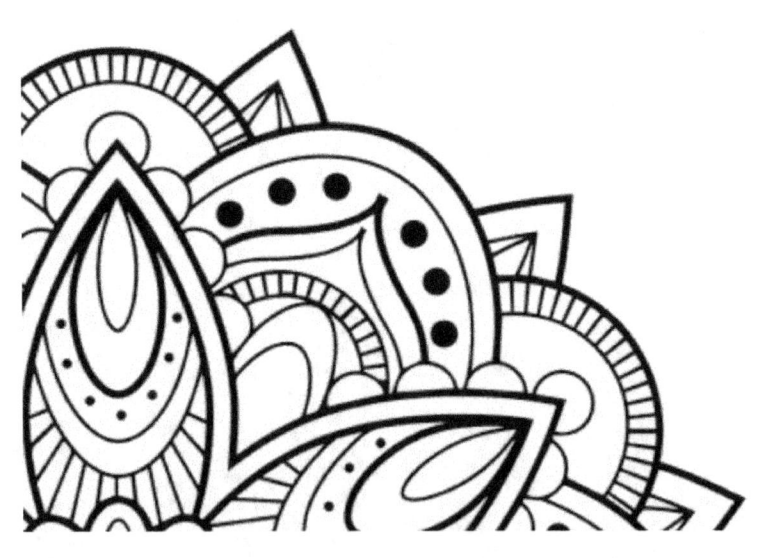

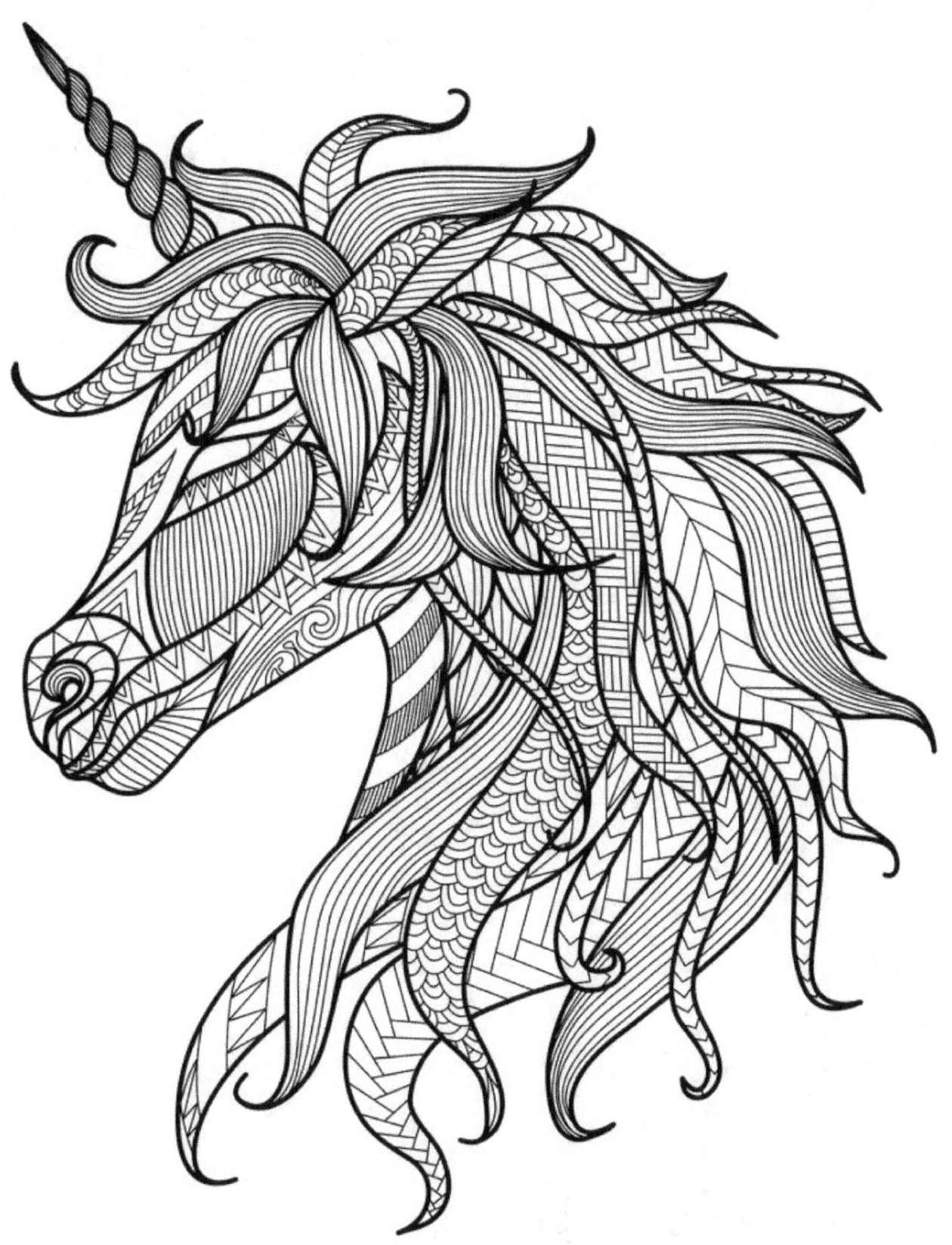

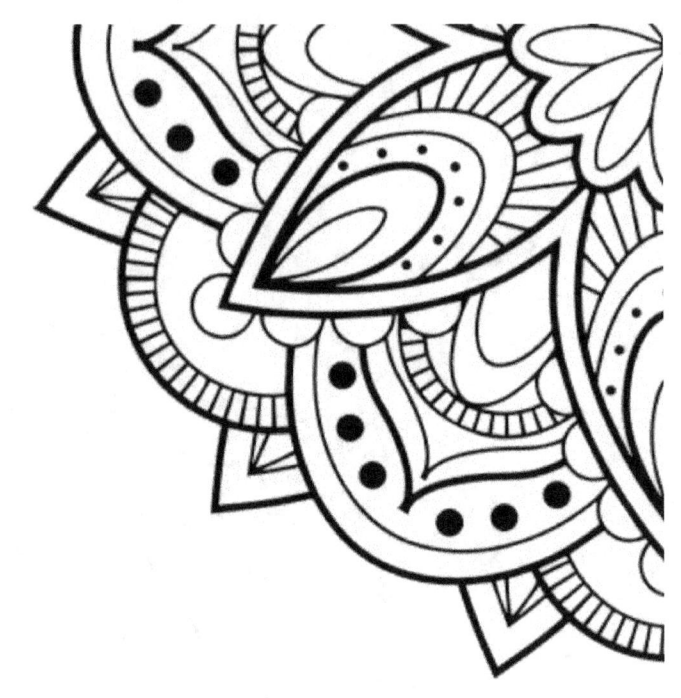

I AM

NOT

A

VICTIM

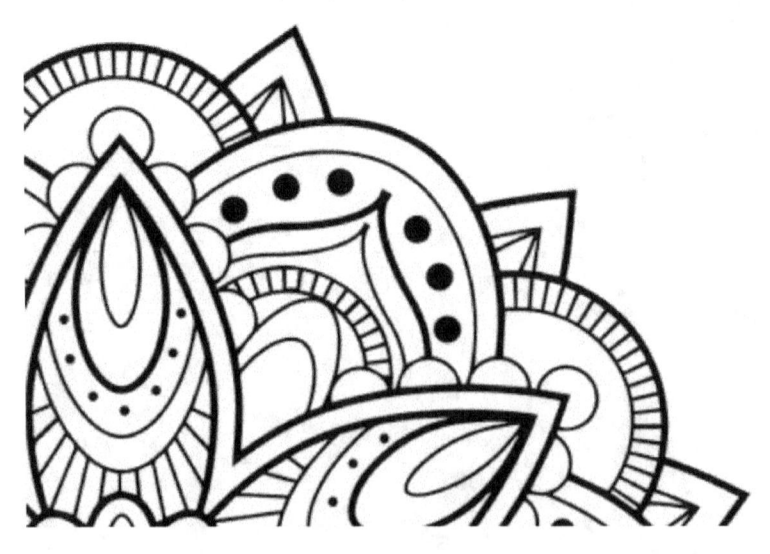

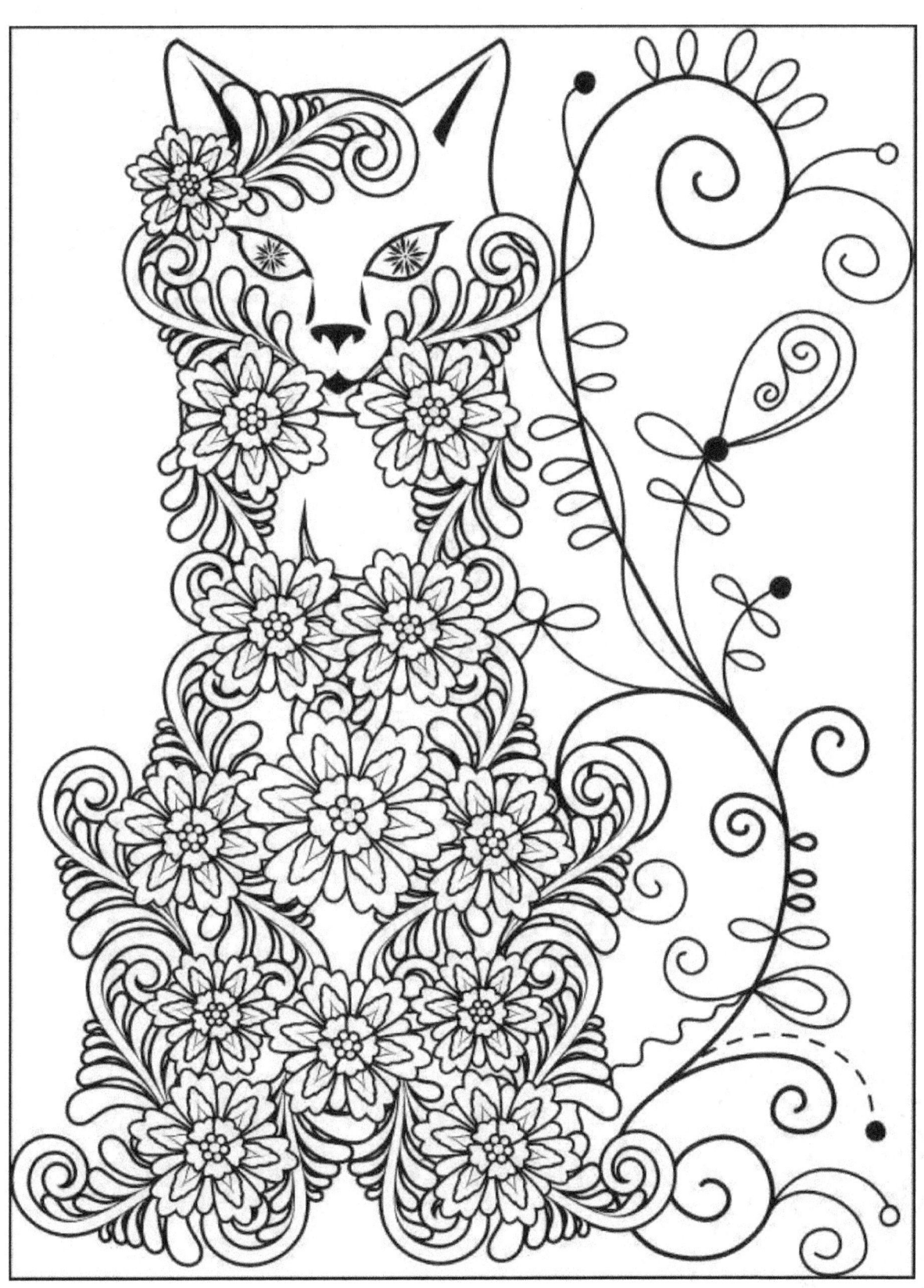

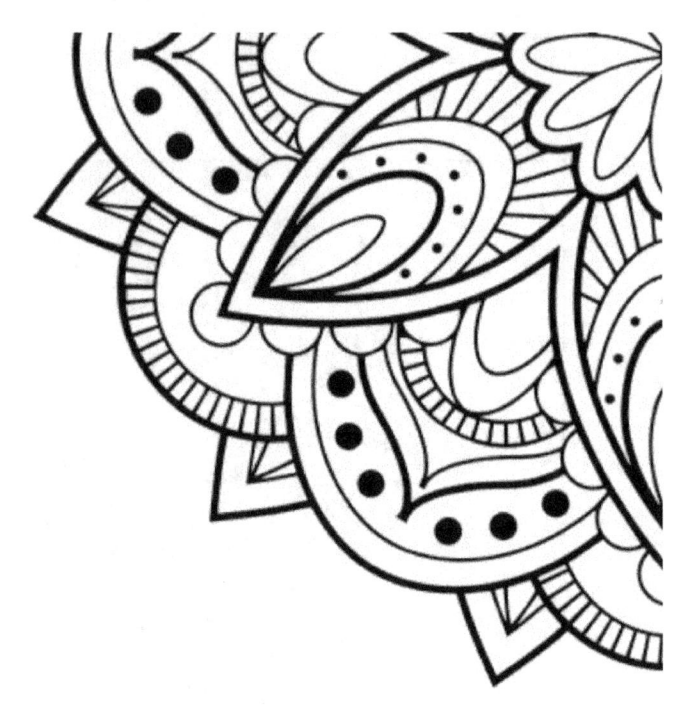

BEING HAPPY
COMES EASY
TO ME

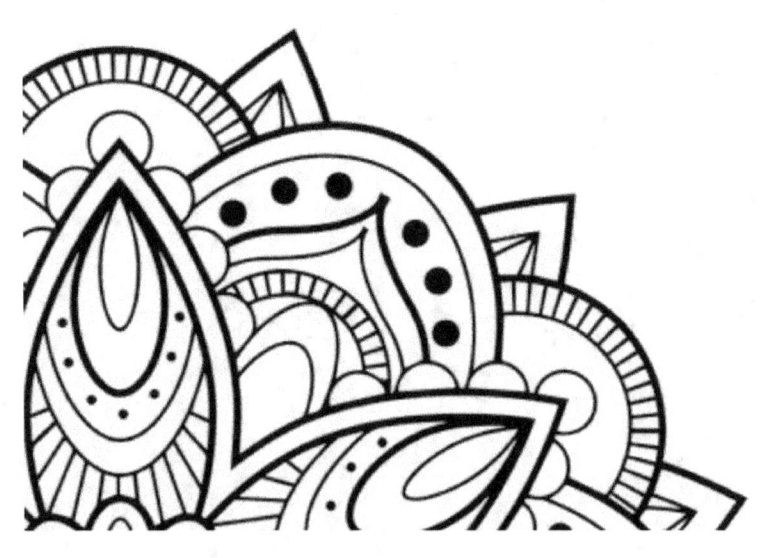

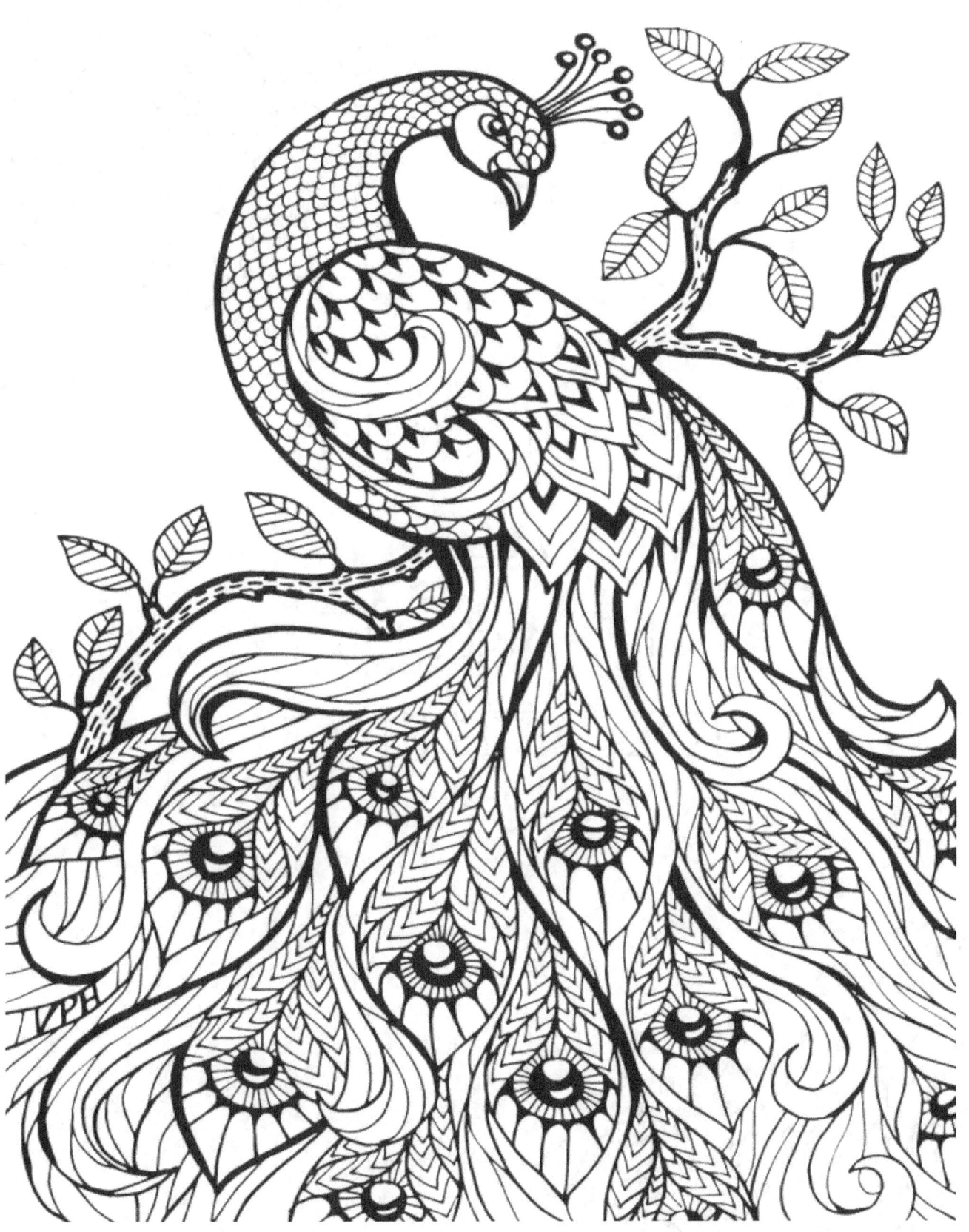

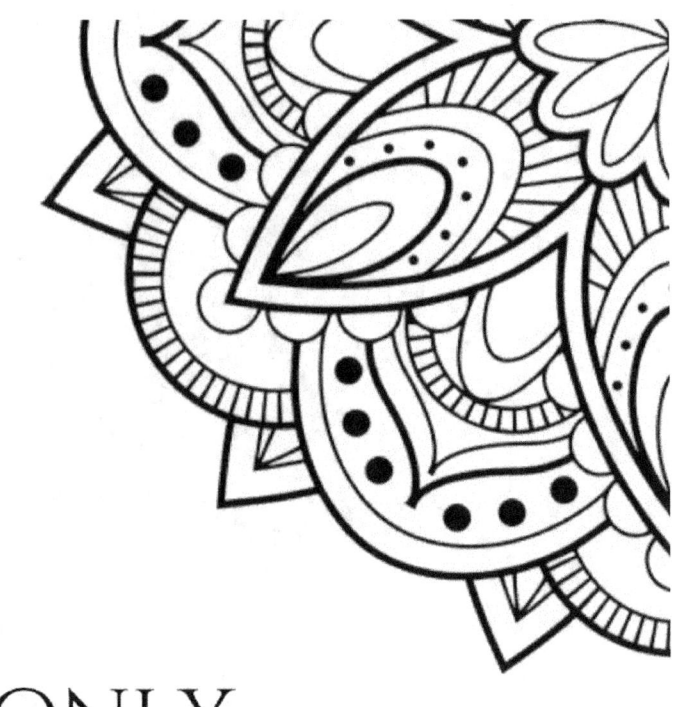

I LOOK ONLY
AT
THE BRIGHT
SIDE OF THINGS

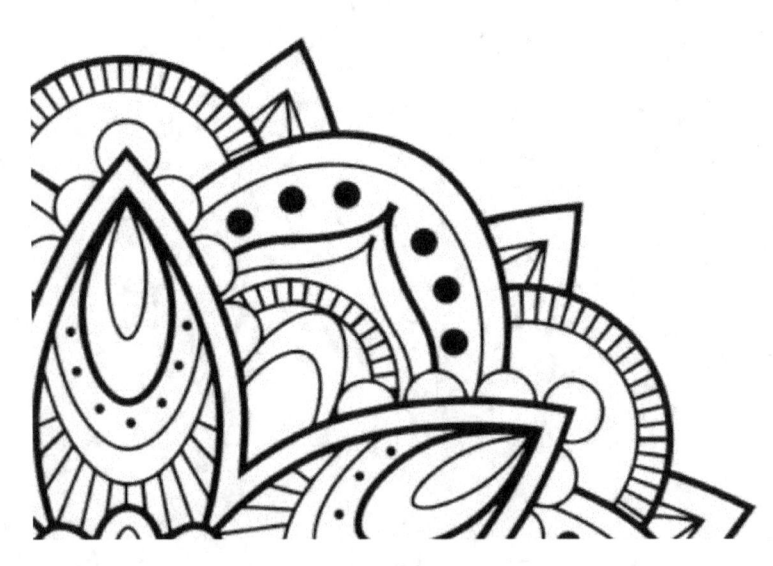

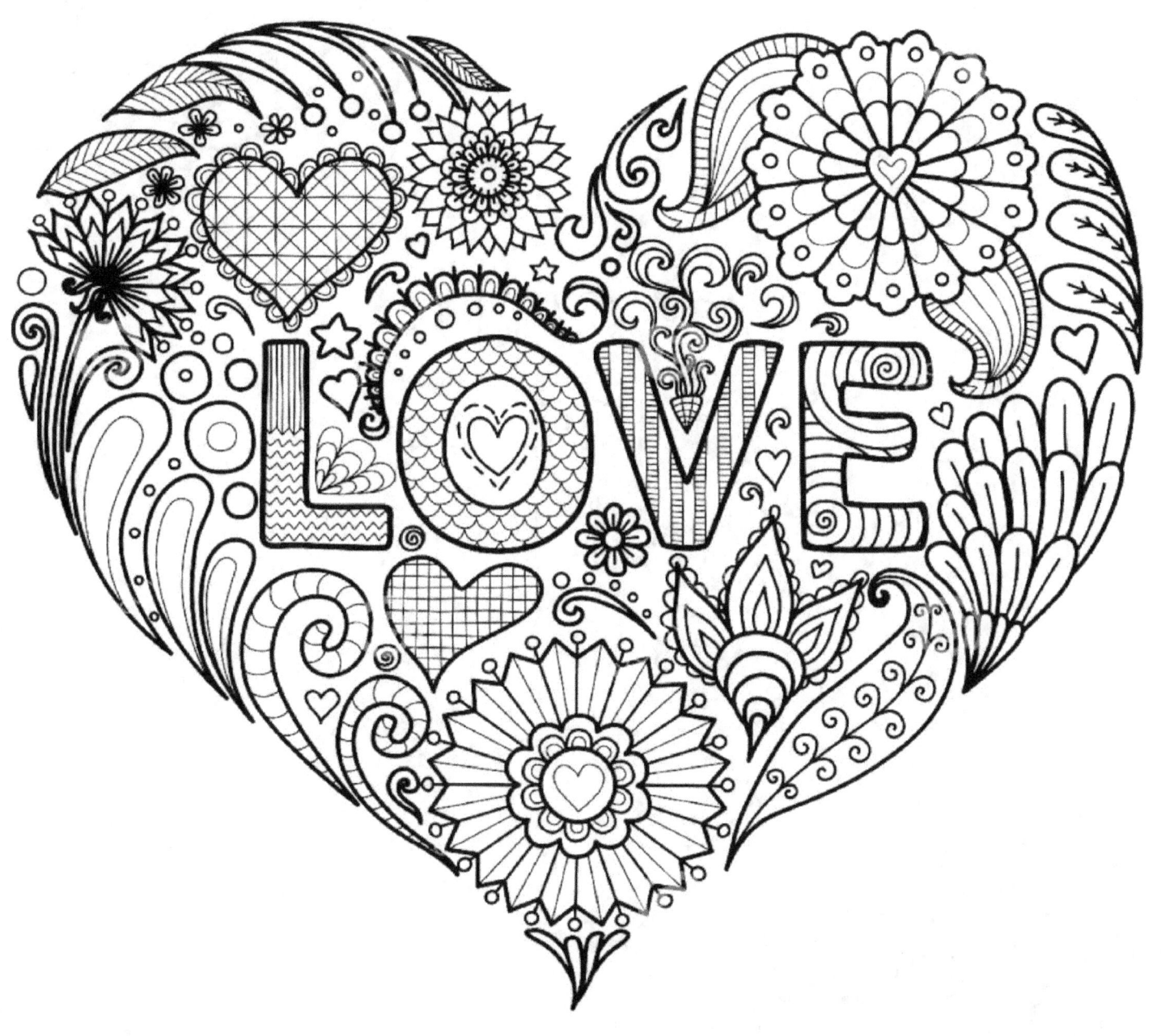

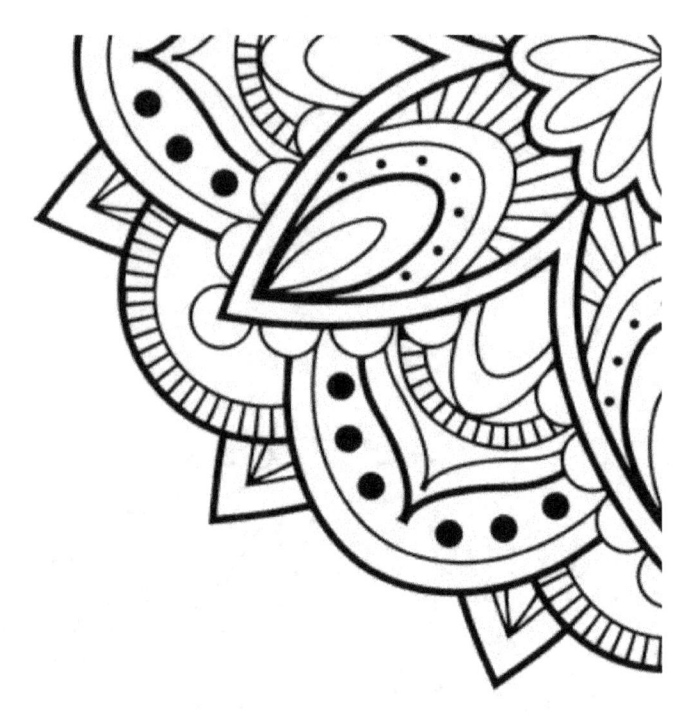

I AM OPEN
TO
NEW BEGINNINGS

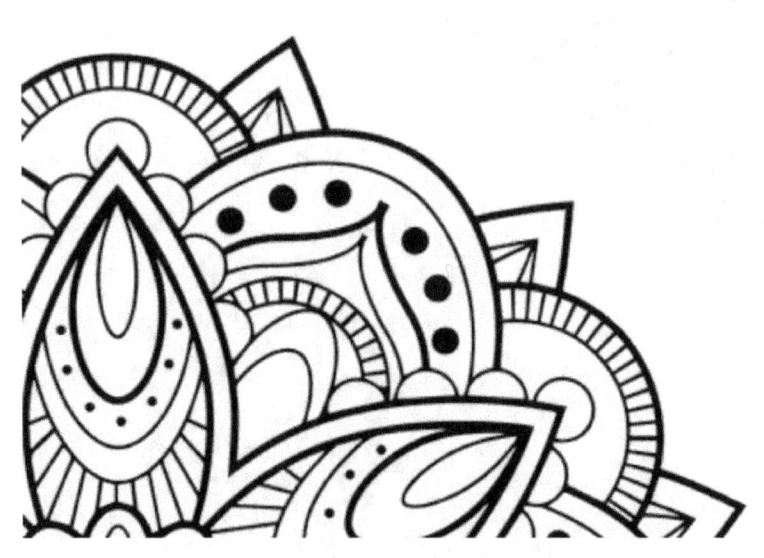

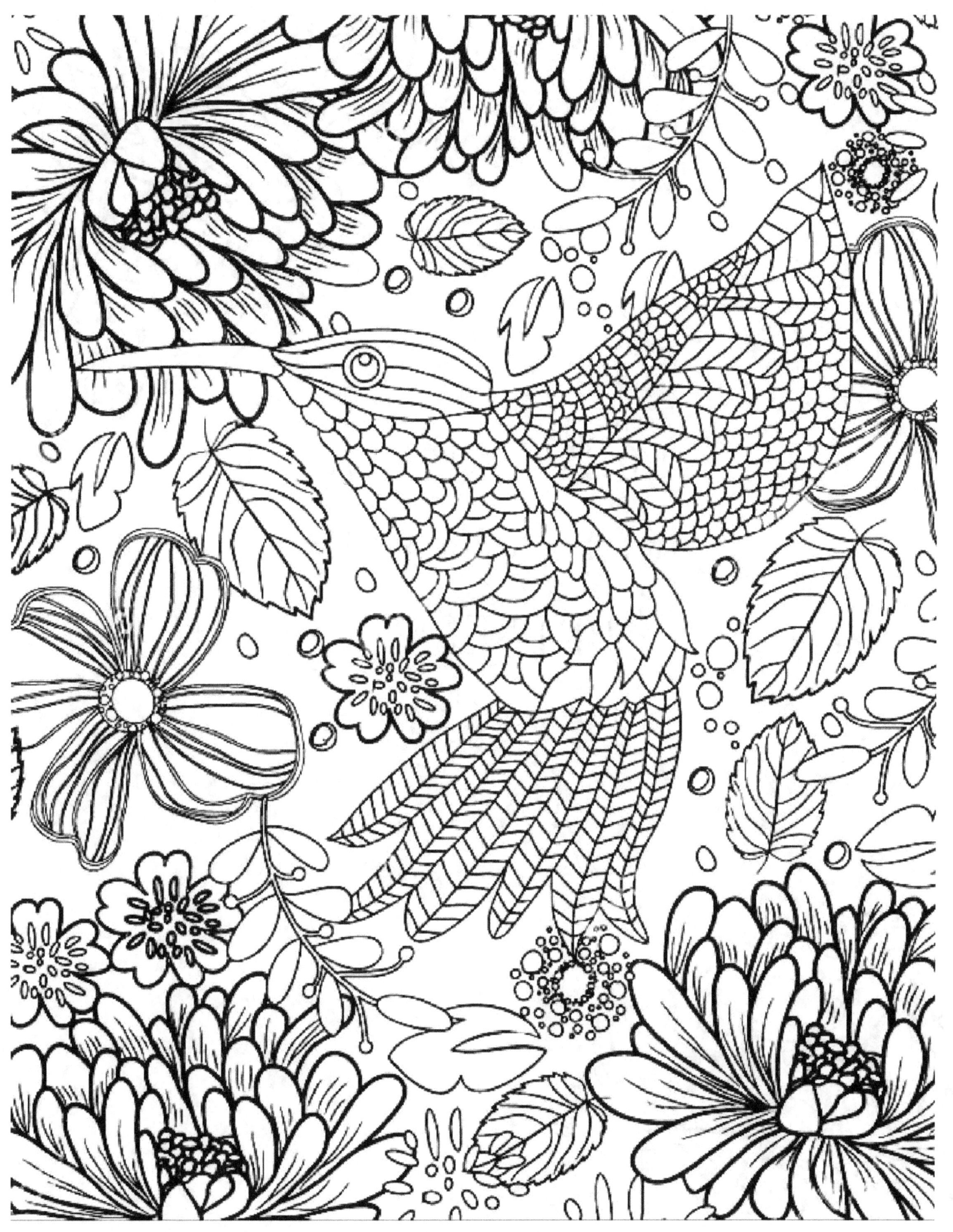

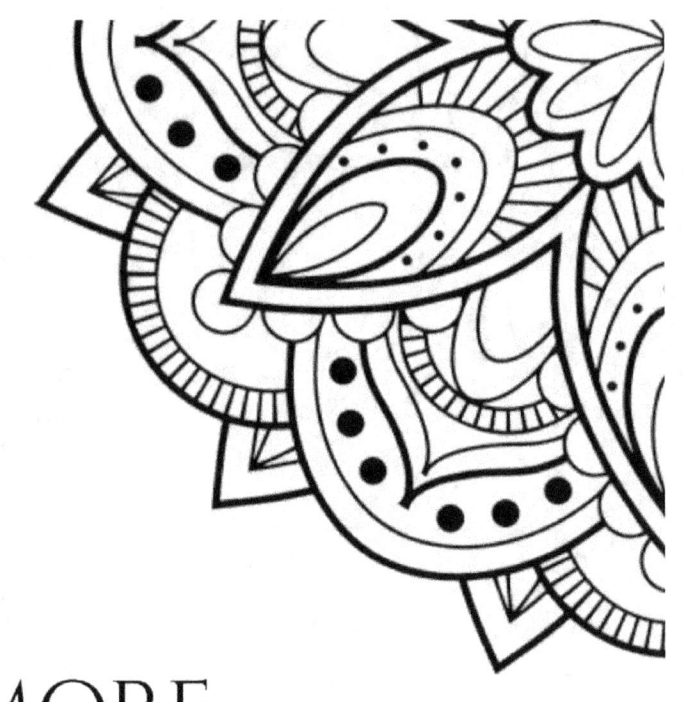

I GIVE MORE
POWER TO MY
PRESENT
THAN MY
PAST

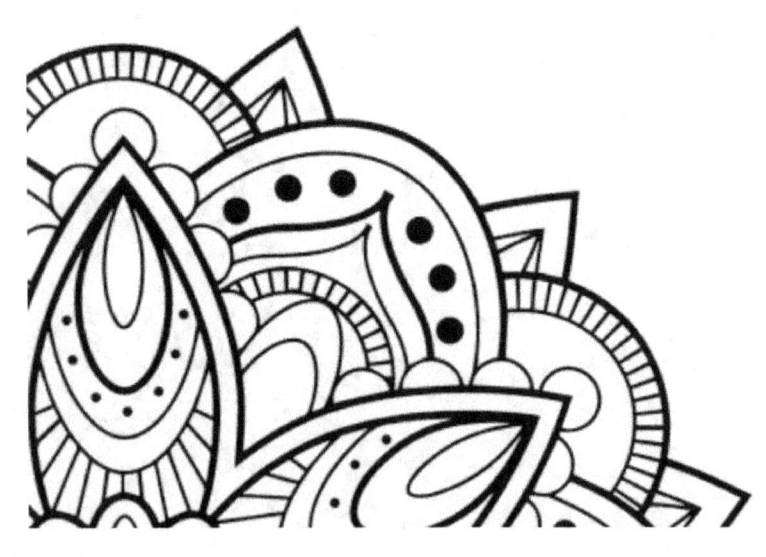

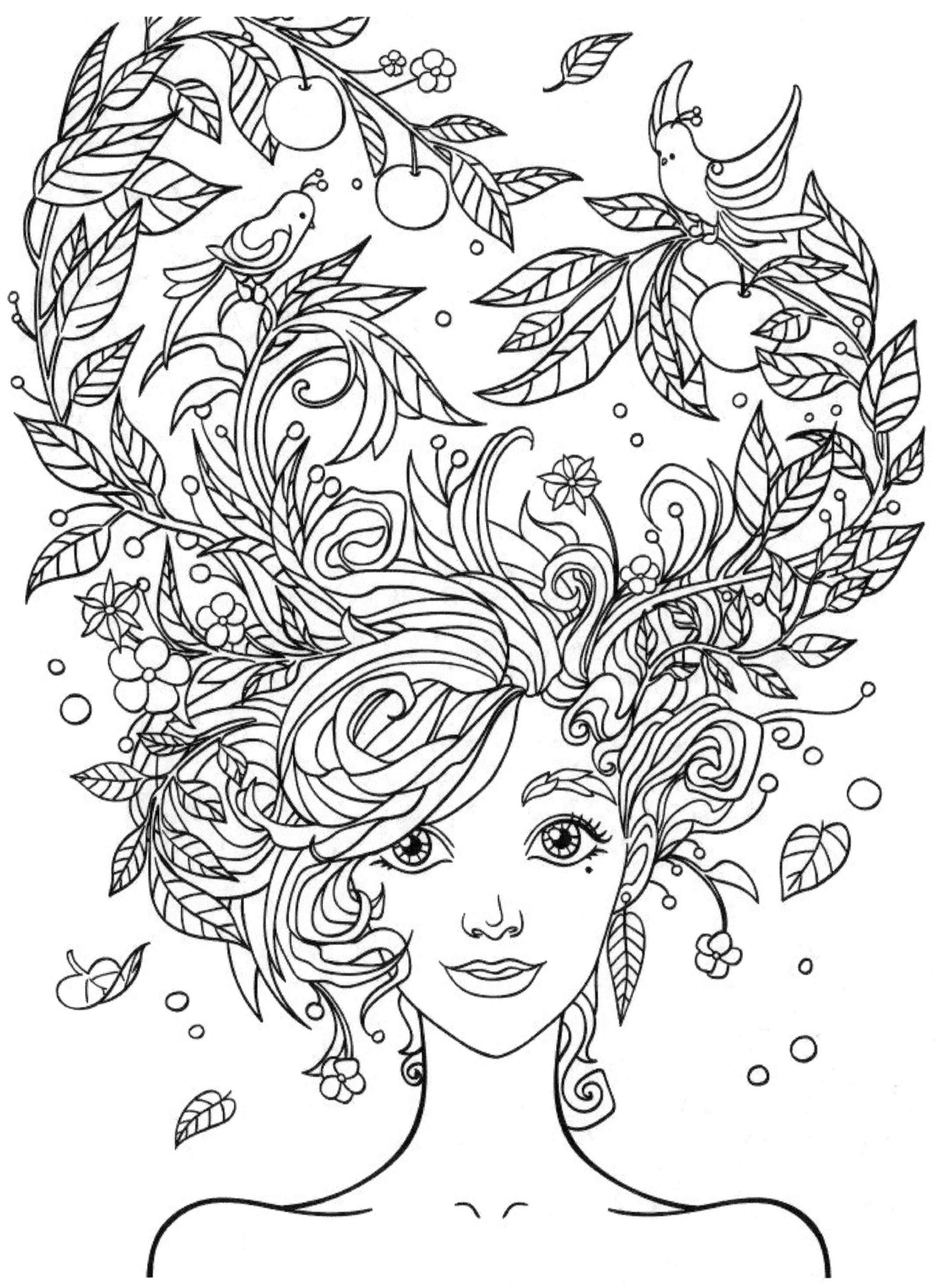

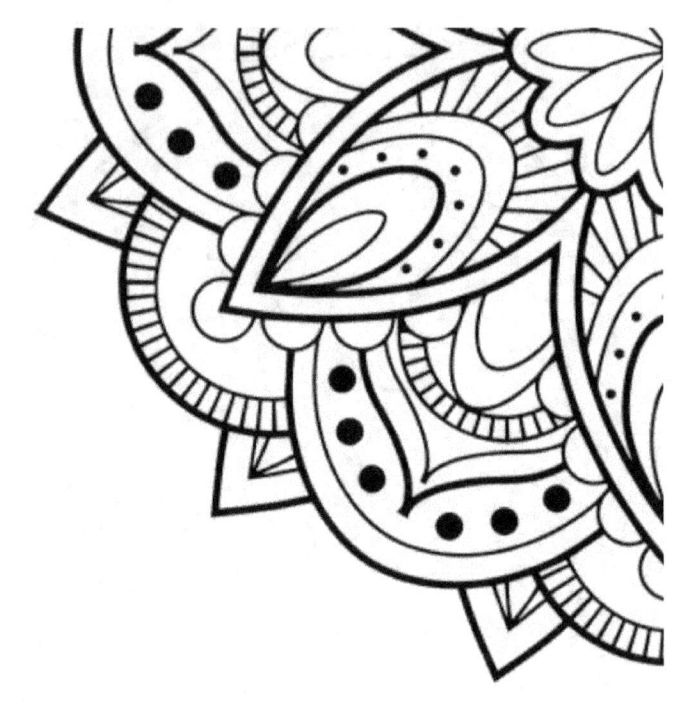

I AM

NOT

STUCK

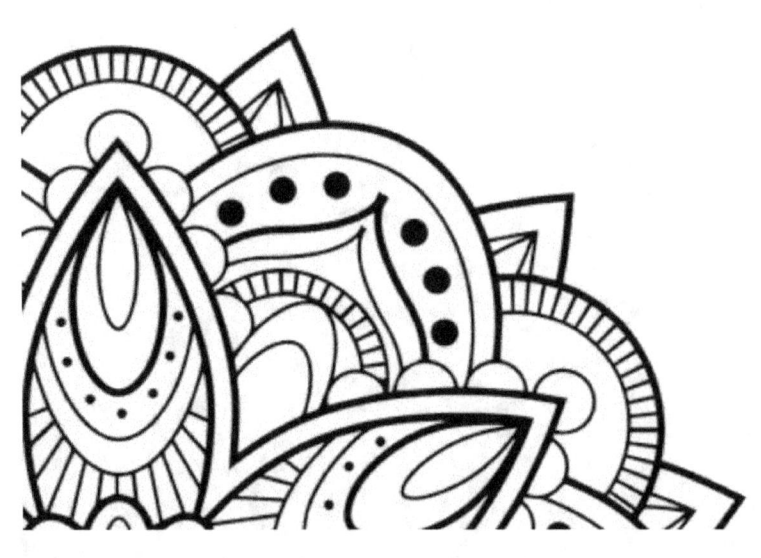

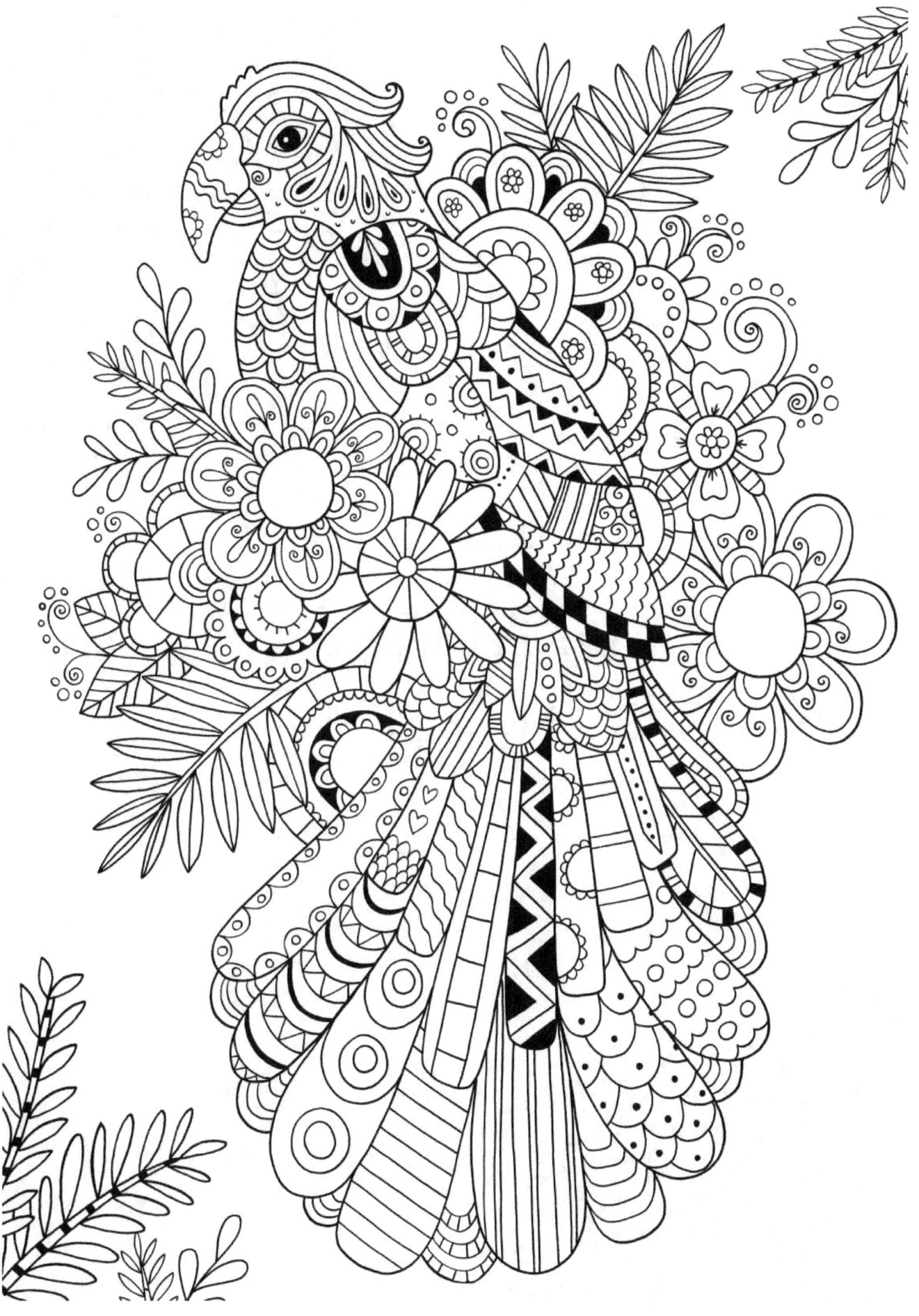

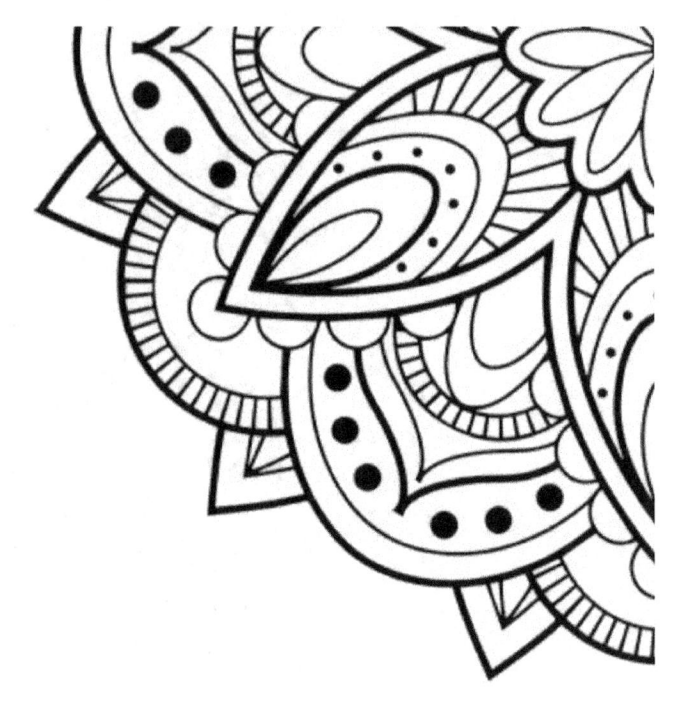

I AM
GRATEFUL
FOR IT
ALL

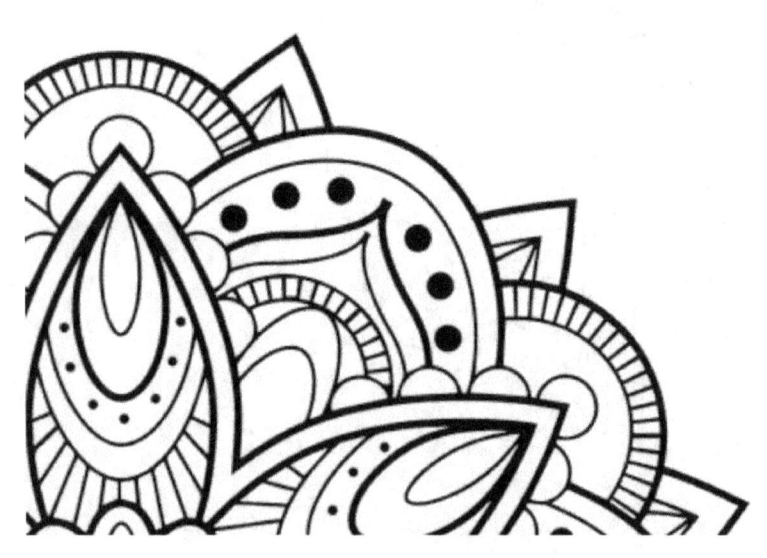

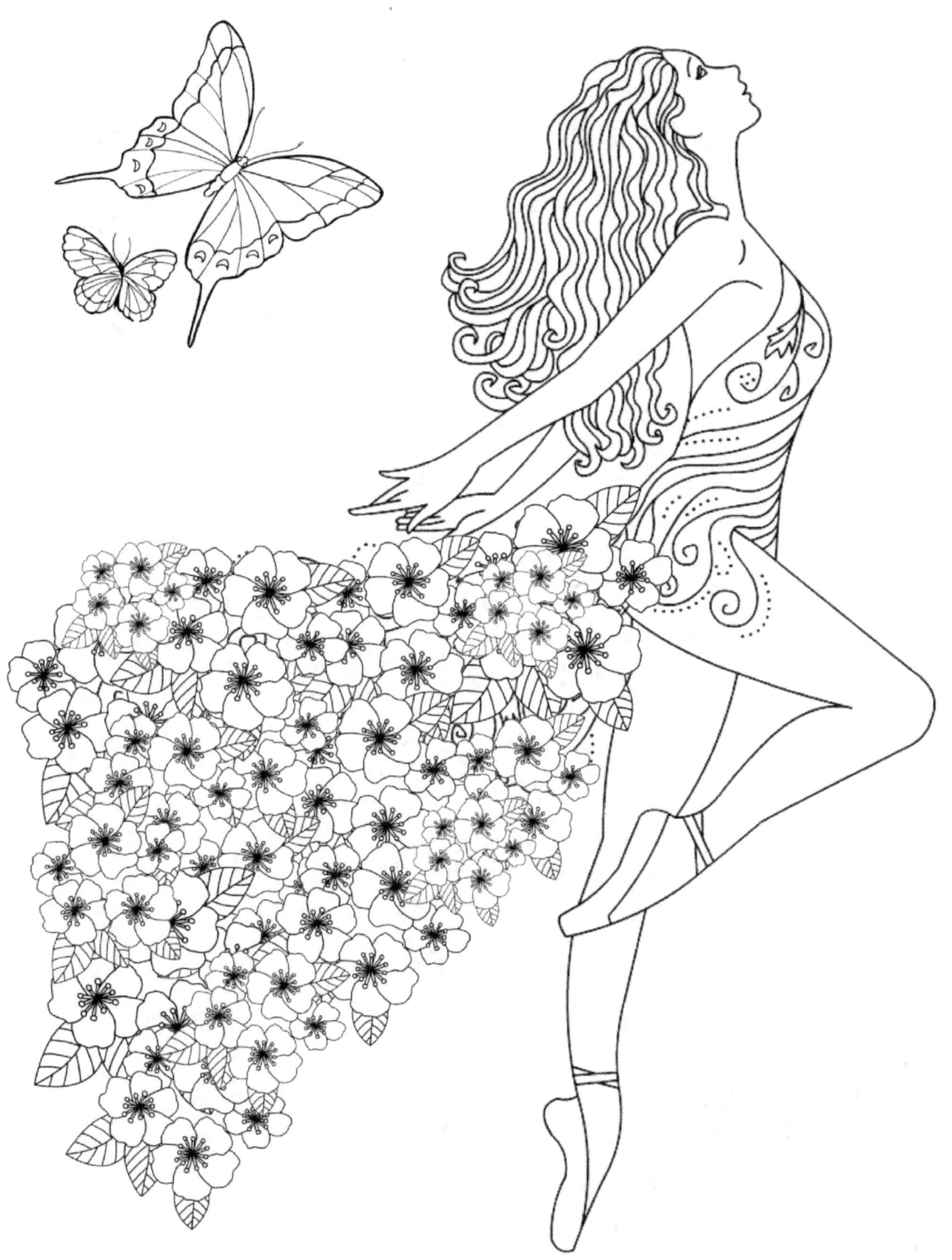

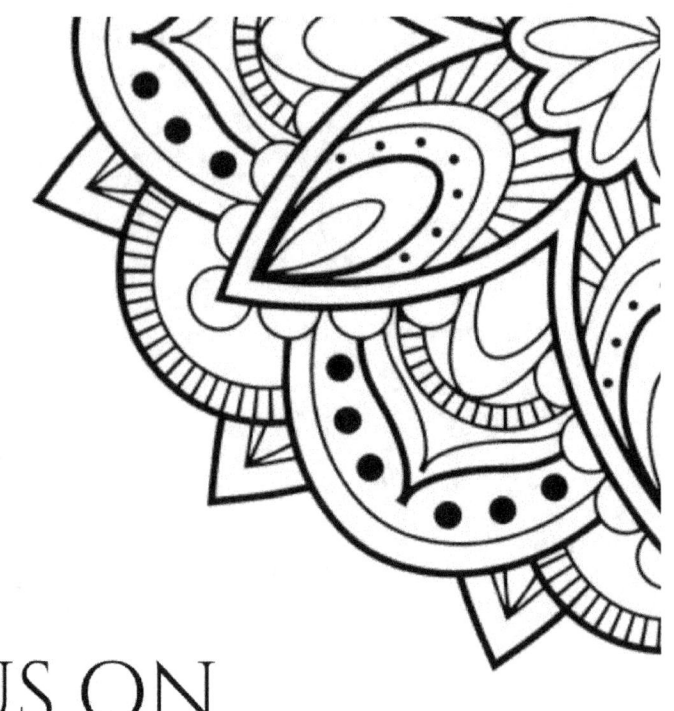

I FOCUS ON
ALL THE
LITTLE THINGS
THAT ARE
WORTH
ENJOYING

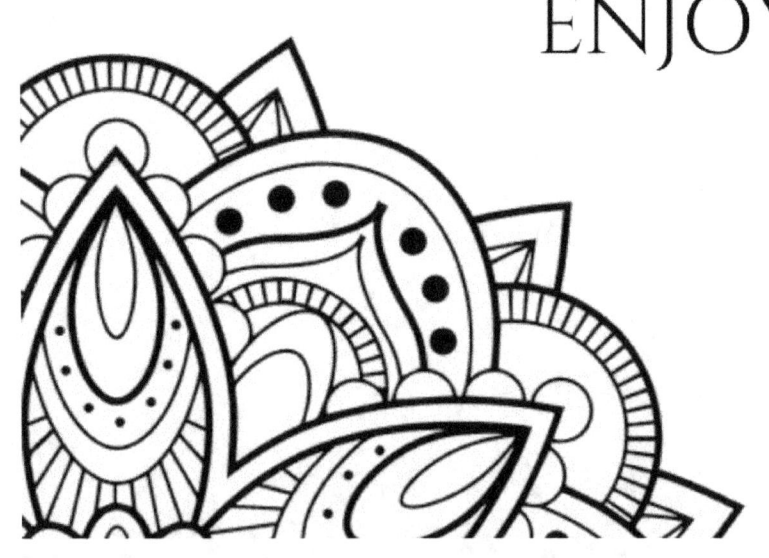

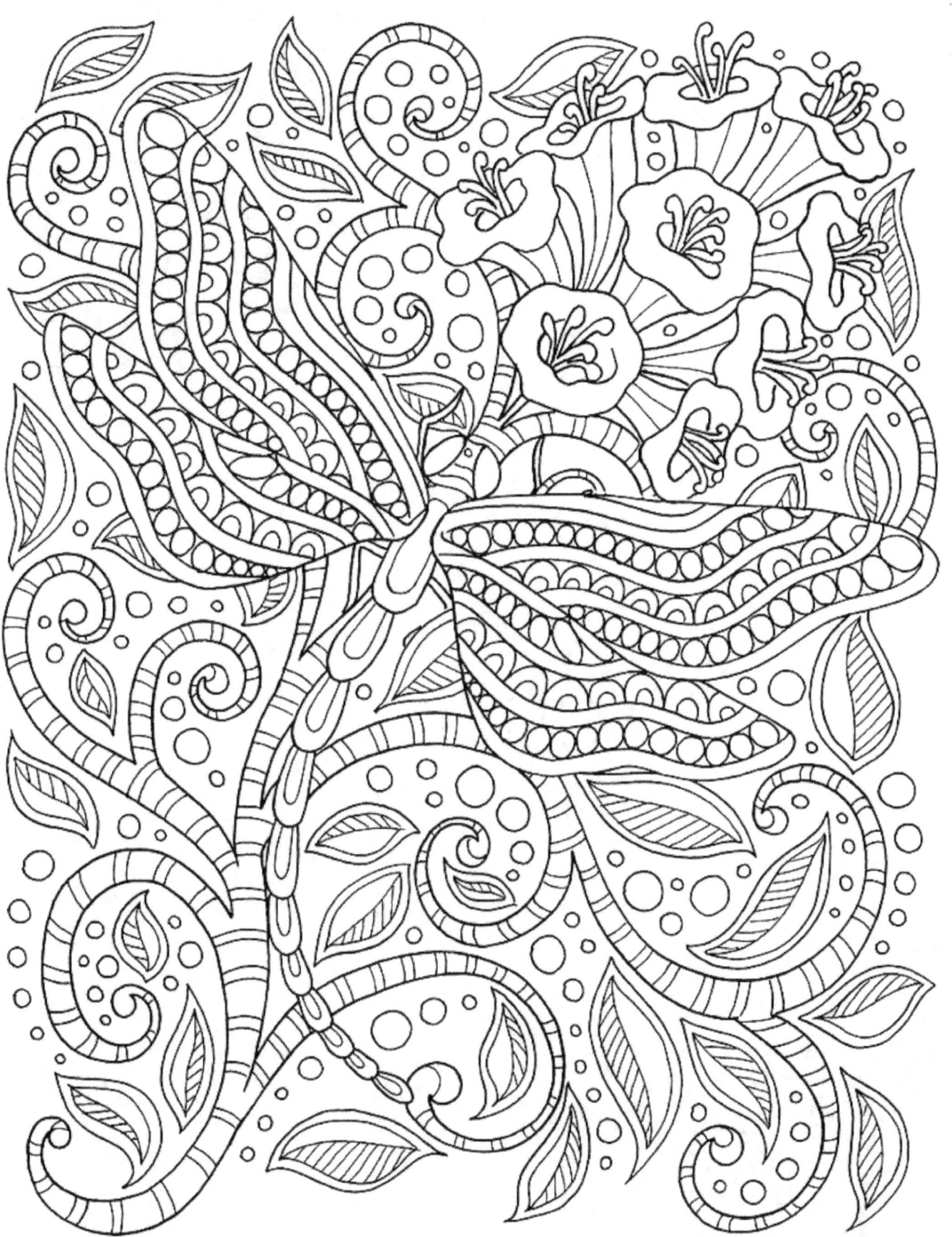

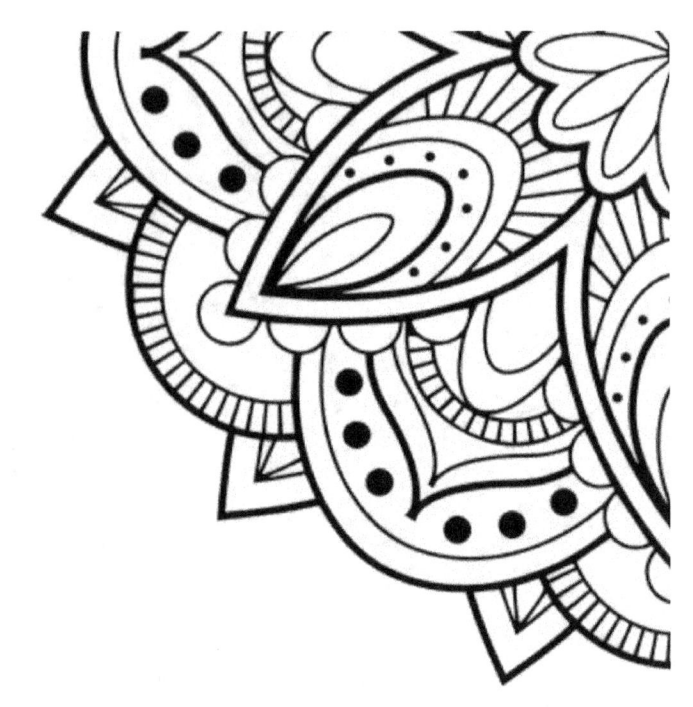

HAPPINESS IS A CHOICE

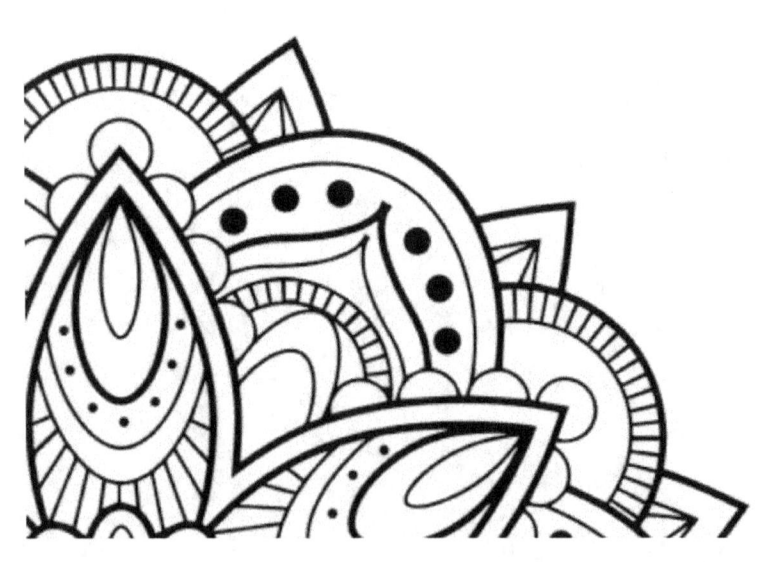

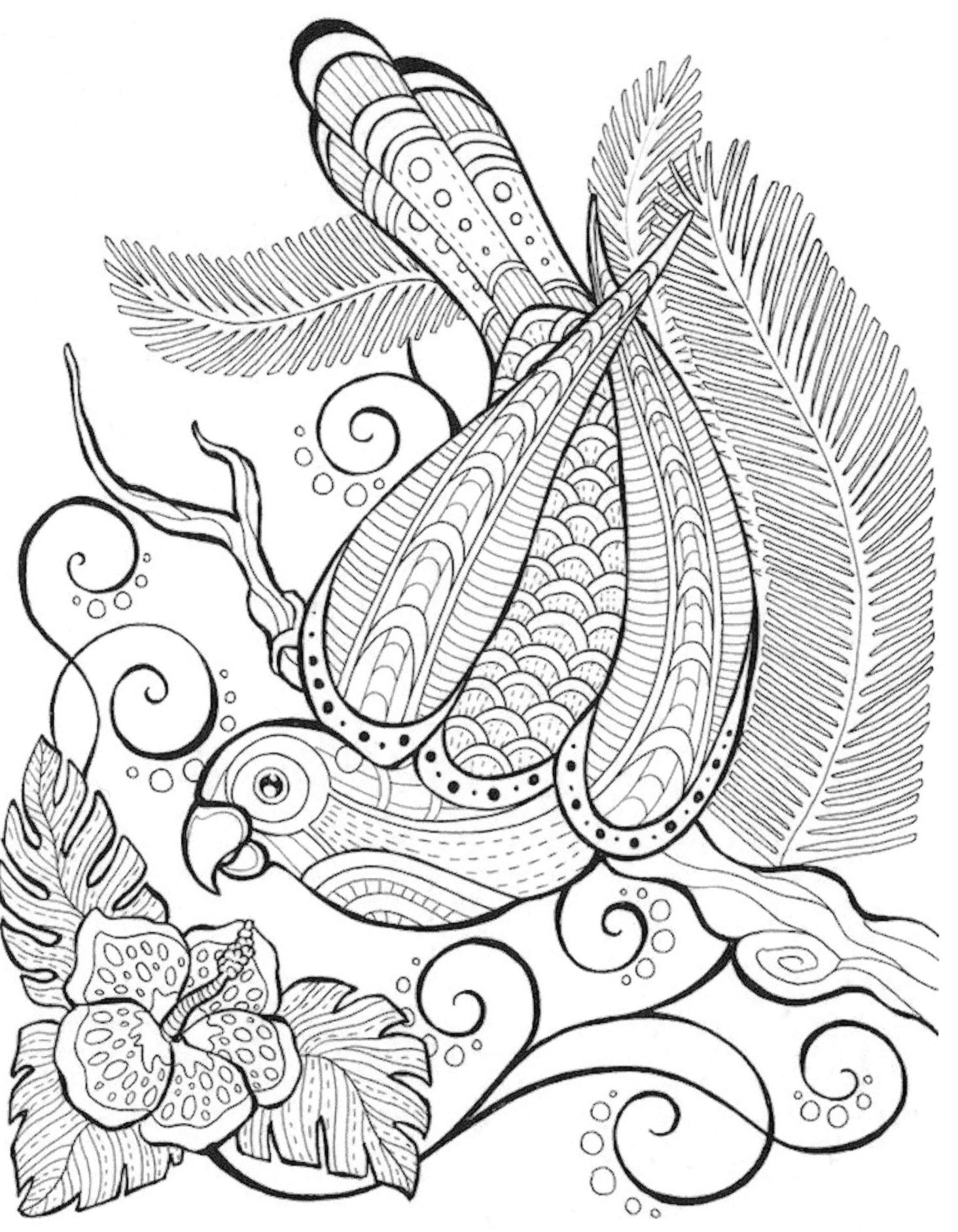

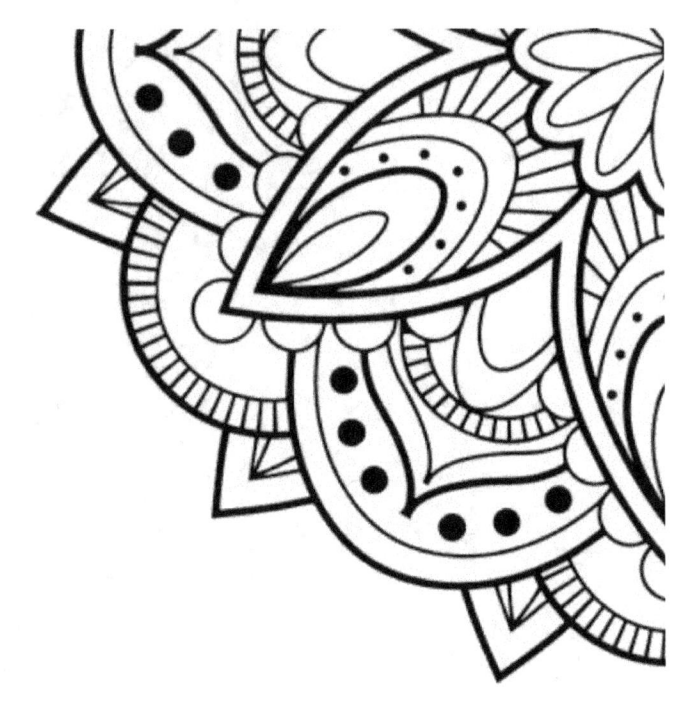

I WILL
CONQUER
MY
CHALLENGES

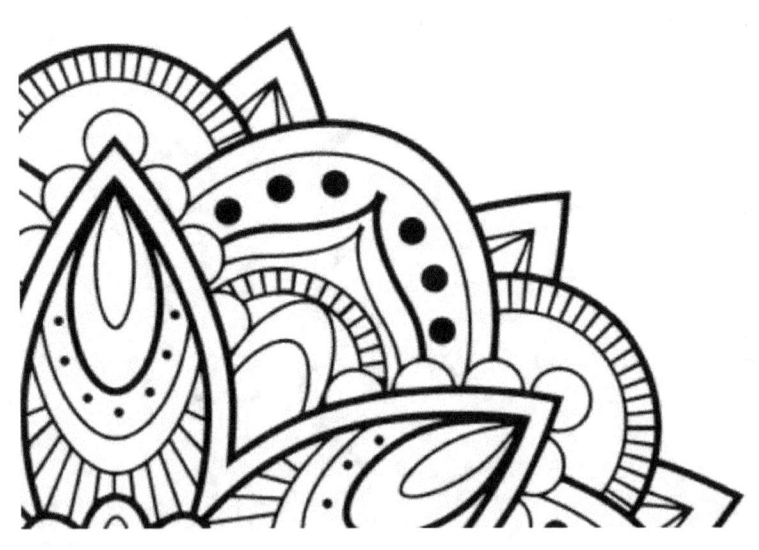

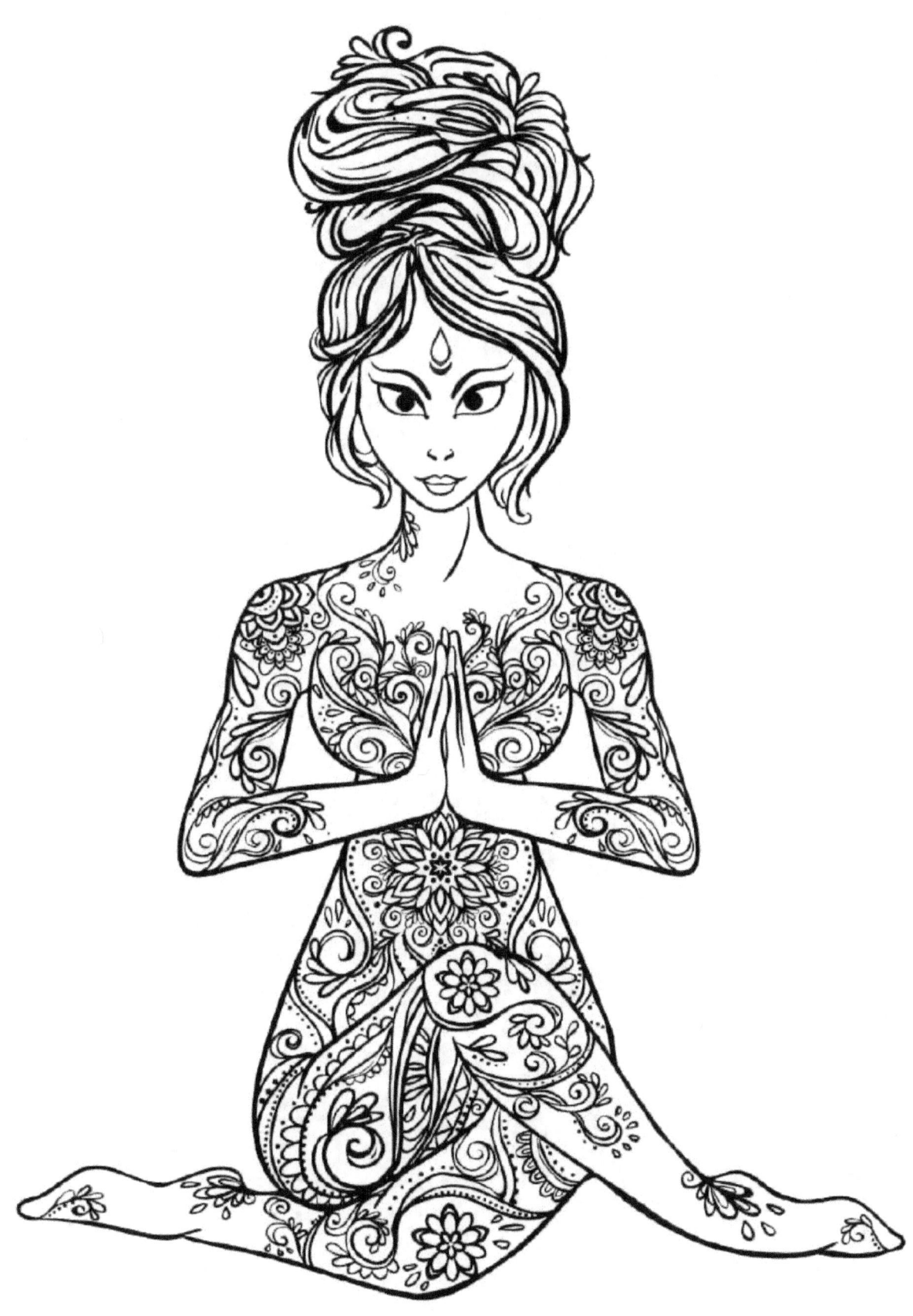